I0160354

How to start over, when life needs a

Factory Reset

Jesus in 20/20, Volume 2

Daniel J. Koren

Koren Creations, LLC
Missouri, USA

Copyright © 2020 Daniel J. Koren

All rights reserved.

ISBN: 978-0-9795291-7-7

Printed in the United States of America

www.Jesusin2020.com

Scripture quotations marked "LITV" come from the *Literal Translation of the Holy Bible*, copyright 1976-2000, Jay P. Green, Sr, used with permission.

Scripture quotes abbreviated as "NKJV" taken from the New King James Version®. Copyright © 1982 by Thomas Nelson. Used by permission. All rights reserved.

Scripture quotations designated "NLT" come from the *Holy Bible*, New Living Translation, copyright © 1996, 2004, 2015 by Tyndale House Foundation. Used by permission of Tyndale House Publishers, Inc., Carol Stream, Illinois 60188. All rights reserved.

Scripture quotations marked "KJV" come from the 1769 King James Version of the Holy Bible (also known as the Authorized Version), public domain.

To

Jesus

who loved me

even with my old operating system

CONTENTS

INTRODUCTION

SOMETHING RIPPED at my guts. Sin and guilt flowed out of me as I wept. I knelt on our living room floor at my children's feet and asked their forgiveness. With a bowl of water and a towel, I humbled myself and washed their feet.

I shouldn't have been on my knees crying like that.

I'd been "saved" for decades.

I was a normal Christian.

I prayed every day.

I read my Bible.

I brought people to Jesus.

I taught others from the Bible.

Yet, I found myself being converted. Jesus had begun something in me the night before. I made things right with my wife for stuff that had happened many years prior. No, I had not run off with another woman or murdered anyone, but I had junk I needed to make right.

The Lord used that conversation to trigger an avalanche in me. I had to confess to my children, too. I had been a harsh parent. A year-long bout with depression had left me self-centered and insensitive to how I treated them.

I sobbed so hard it was tough to get air.

Perhaps they did not all understand why I was weeping, washing their feet, and drying them that morning during our normal devotion time. But we all sensed that something was changing.

I was being reset.

God had designed original factory specs for my life but I had been living by a different operating system. He wanted me living by the power of joy, peace, and hope. I amped off adrenaline, anger, and intimidation.

I hid my sin behind the idea that I wasn't as bad as some guys and I had done a lot of things right. Still, my rage, stress, and impatience were unacceptable. Not only was I living from the wrong source, I was training them to feed off the wrong motivations.

I can't trace exactly what flipped that switch. Jesus used a serious point made by a comedian to trigger something in my thinking, which snowballed into an avalanche inside me. The resulting life-change was more than an emotional fit.

My thinking took a turn. My actions followed. I began putting my family's needs ahead of mine. I made myself vulnerable to them.

This book is not about family relationships but about getting life on the right track one every level. Are you ready to be reset? Someone at death's door is usually ready for anything. Someone who has suffered a divorce or a death might be ready to be reset, but what about the people rocking along happily through life?

When God grabbed me, I was doing well, considering. What changed me? Seeing Jesus. I had begun to look at Him not just as a religious/spiritual connection, but a friend. Someone who had access to every secret of my life.

I mentioned a little about how I changed in my book *Seeing Jesus*. Here, I've shared a little more. But this isn't about me and Jesus. It is about you. Will you discover how to live from the right motivations? Are you willing to question yourself?

Jesus came to reset us. All of us. Not just drunks and prostitutes, but religious people, too. Many of the Bible-readers of His time were not ready for the upheaval He brought, and they hated Him.

If you are like them, you will hate this book.

But if you know that things are just not right, if you long to be exactly what God designed you to be, keep turning the pages. Jesus will speak to you. He will flip something inside you even if you thought you were perfect.

Hang on for the ride. It might be painful to delete corrupted thinking and default triggers. The fresh install, however, is a rewarding experience you will never regret. If you let Him do His work, you will compute differently, respond correctly to upsets in life, and have a default for good instead of evil.

I recommend that you read one chapter of this book each day. It will take you about a month at that pace. You can binge-read it in one day if you like. However, the message will soak in better and last for the long term if taken in small doses.

Be sure you obtain the *Handbook for Your Factory Reset* to record your new insights and chart your growth in the Lord. It loosely follows the sequence of this book. As you read the selected Scriptures from the Gospels, notate the changes inside you each day. Print off the free PDF you can download from Jesusin2020.com/handbook2 or buy the paperback from that site or the online Amazon store.

FOREWORD

IN THE FIRST BOOK of this series (*Seeing Jesus*), we learned that Jesus's ministry was in prelaunch. We've met Andrew, Peter, John, Phillip, Nathanael, and others and saw that they were in a "trial membership," so to speak. Discipleship begins as "come and see" long before it becomes "go and do." They were simply close to Jesus, getting to know Him better.

That is why you are reading this book. I'm so excited that we are continuing the journey. So many people expressed what a big difference the first book in this series made in their lives.

Too many believers skip the step of just getting close to Jesus. To the first followers He was a person. To us, He could be a church thing. A topic. A belief system.

The closer they looked at this "friend," they realized He was "Messiah," "King," and "Son of God." They were not just casual onlookers. What is He to you?

To the seekers who saw Jesus, He said, "Follow Me."[1] If you already read *Seeing Jesus*, then I assume you are here

---

[1] See John 1:43.

4

because you want to follow Him, too. What did it mean to those common citizens when Jesus said that, though?

You could mash the blue "follow" on my bookFace page, or I could follow you on Tweeter or Instagrab. While I would be glad to see you on social media, that idea of "following" does not involve commitment. Even when you do "follow" a person online, many of his or her posts will not show up in your newsfeed. (Sigh.)

That idea of following was foreign to the minds of those Galileans. To "follow" a rabbi was to walk behind him. There, you could observe all he did and said. The followers would be watching and learning so they could duplicate him later.

In this volume, step in stride with the sandaled feet from Galilee. Let's get to know Him and let Him change us. A routine life will be upset with this *Factory Reset*.

On your mark!

Ready?

Get reset!

WATCHFUL WEDDING

HAVE YOU EVER had a smart phone with corrupted files or that was loaded with junk you didn't need? Maybe apps would lock it up or the screen would freeze at random moments. Often, I have restarted my phone to try and fix buggy issues. However, there's been a few times my phone needed a factory reset.

I like when a phone manufacturer produces a better version of their software. I like to do a fresh install and enjoy the faster apps and smoother zooming and swooshing on the screen. (Sorry, I don't have the technical words for that stuff.)

In life, we all need a reset from the Maker. We were born with corrupted software. We were born in sin and random impressions in our early lives led us to more sin. He did not design us to be powered by fear, rage, or shame, but somehow by adulthood such vices become our defaults.

I sat next to a man in grad school who had installed Android software on an Apple phone (or maybe it was the other way around). I have often wondered how well that worked, which features were unavailable, and if he was happy with that decision. I can think of all kinds of potential problems such a

6

phone would have—and I have enough trouble with smartphones as it is!

God created human hardware. Sadly, the software files have been corrupted. The factory settings in your life and mine default toward the wrong things. If we are ever going to function correctly, we have to let the Maker do a factory reset of our lives.

Too often we assume our religion, experience, and knowledge are original equipment. Jesus challenges us to see through His eyes, to be reset from above and live by the default settings of His realm. If you let it, this journey will change parts of your life that you cannot put words to.

Jesus used a wedding as a moment to illustrate the massive reset He was bringing to earth. That drastic change began for a few who were there. A person who experiences the Master's reset can never be what he or she once was.

Jesus's disciples followed Him to a family event.[2] The disciples were still in the "come and see" mode of watching the Master. They did not have official responsibilities yet.

Too many believers skip this step of getting close to Jesus. Many of us heard the gospel as a remedy rather than a relationship. So, we did what someone told us to do to "get saved."

Because of the power of the Gospel, we felt good and refreshed with a new spiritual force at work in our lives. But Christianity is not like a diet or weight-loss program that helps you feel better and more energetic because of wise changes you make in your life. It is a friendship.

---

[2] Acts 1:21-22 indicates that the core 12 were all influenced by John before meeting Jesus. Those 12 and others could have been following Him as early as this event in Cana, but they are not officially chosen until months later.

Coming to Jesus should feel like you have met the most amazing person and you are willing to change up everything in your life to be with Him. That's what these followers did. All they knew was that Jesus was unlike anyone they had ever met and they did not want to be anywhere but with Him.

Not only had the Rabbi allowed His new followers to see His home, He took them in as family. When one of Mary's family members had a wedding, the invitation included Jesus and His disciples.[3] Already, the disciples have become family.[4] They all headed to Cana, a town in Galilee.

Weddings can be fun. Weddings can be stressful. This event gave the new followers a chance to observe their Rabbi in a different setting.

At a typical feast, including weddings, guests would contribute to the meal. Think crockpots and covered dishes today. No doubt Jesus and this recently gained tribe put a dent in the refreshments. I worry that their RSVP's did not arrive before this hungry group did.

Remember now, Jesus had recently gone 40 days without eating. I wouldn't blame Him if He took a second plate or two. Since they had all just walked for a whole day to get there, they had reason for big appetites and great thirst.

Somewhere between eating the homemade rolls and the serving of the triple-chocolate cake,[5] something went wrong. The wedding consultant was panicking. The bride was in tears. Mary realized the problem: the punch bowl was empty.

She brought the problem to Jesus.

---

[3] See John 2:1-2.
[4] John 2:1 could mean they had only known Jesus for three days!
[5] Nah, they didn't have all that.

Yeah, yeah, I know. We should all bring our problems to Jesus. But I also get what Mary is doing here. At least, I think I do.

My firstborn son is handy at fixing everything. Whether something needs welding, a photo needs to be retouched, or we want to retexture and paint the living room, he's my main man. When something goes wrong around my house, I call my engineering/creative firstborn to bail me out. So, I sympathize with Mary in this crisis. She goes to her Firstborn.

"We have a problem." Mary says, "They have no wine."[6]

Wait. Jesus's first training of His team is at a drinking party? You mean to tell me Jesus says, "Watch this," and then brings them to a place where liquor is served with minors present? What are we following here anyway?

Calm down. It's not what you think.

You, as well as I, have seen the damage alcohol can cause. Alcoholism has destroyed the lives of friends of mine who grew up with parents ruled by its power. So, it is understandable and right for us to be concerned that some would use an event like this to validate their addiction.

Alcohol can bypass logic centers in a person's brain. Often, they become driven by emotion, thinking from the limbic cortex like a young child. The reflexes and impulses from that region do not filter through one's morals, personal values, or a sense of consequences. Thus, people under the influence of alcohol often feel shame and regret once they are sober and realize what they have done.

Jesus does not want us going back to primal stages of immaturity. He wants to reset us to the core, not leave us to be

---

[6] John 2:3, LITV. The first quote in this paragraph is my own paraphrase of what she was thinking if not actually saying.

victims of a broken system. There is more to life than impulse and regret![7]

Mary knew her family should provide their fair share of the refreshments at this week-long feast. She simply presented Jesus with the problem. Jesus responded, "What is that to Me and to you, woman? My hour has not yet come."[8]

Well, no one said family wasn't messy. We tiptoe away from that conversation thinking, "Awkward!" Again, it is not as bad as it sounds. Jesus loves her and even in His dying moments called her "Woman" while making sure she was provided for and protected. I would never say to my mom, "Look here, woman," because in our culture that is disrespectful. It is more like Jesus says, "Why are you involving Me in this, ma'am?"

Remember, Jesus has come to flip over our lives. Mary's needed to be reset, too. Jesus is challenging her to belief, challenging her to follow Him. How does He provoke her? By responding to her request with a question. Why did she ask Him? Was she aware of what His "hour" was?

We can imagine that for the past 30 years, Mary had given those "one of these days you will do great things, son" talks to Jesus. She wanted to see Him step out and do whatever it was He was to do. She did not understand what all that meant though.

Now, the one who submitted at age 12, as much as says, "Your concerns are not My concerns. I have something else I am working toward." It was time to be about His Father's business, not His mother's.

Jesus knew that revealing His identity would hasten His death: "My hour has not arrived yet." Therefore, He could not draw a lot of attention to Himself. Yet. When His "hour" to die came, He would be very active and very open about His

---

[7] See the Appendix A: Alcohol and the Bible

[8] John 2:4, LITV.

identity—even to the point of making the opposition have no other option but to kill Him. But we will get to all of that in good time.

Jesus to Mary: "How is this my concern?"

Mary to household servants: "Whatever He says to you, do."[9]

I just see her throwing her hands up as she says this, as if, "I'm not going to argue about this, but I know He can do something here." She wouldn't stop at His gentle resistance.

It looks like she got the hint about this not be a revealing moment for Him. She kept the operation on the down low, whispering orders to the servants. There is a lesson here for those of us who would follow Jesus. Whatever He says to you do it. And don't make a scene.

You have already had those "Whatever He says, I'll do it" moments. I believe that is why you are here studying this with me. You will do more, much more.

What prompted this "whatever He says" moment? A crisis. Imagine if you had 100 people over at your place and your plumbing backed up or you didn't have drinks for them all. For this young couple to run out of punch, it was social suicide. Yes, it was embarrassing, but it was more than that. A wedding was a celebration of God's favor. This humiliation was more than just poor planning, in a superstitious/religious way it would be seen as an omen about them.

Jesus cares about weddings. He's planning one, too—His own. He couldn't stand by and let this one crash and burn while He was there. He would put the missing part back in this party.

Next we see some unusual furnishings: "there were six stone waterpots standing, according to the purification of the

---

9 John 2:5, LITV.

11

Jews."[10] Galilee was heavily influenced by the Pharisees, who attempted to keep all of Torah perfectly. They did purifying washings like those done at the Temple so that nothing would be defiled. Although those codes of washing utensils and tools did not apply to every home, the devout ones took the commands personally.[11] This home and the people at this feast apparently had hearts to be pure before the Lord.

They used stone barrels to hold the water because stone could not become religiously impure. They often had to destroy clay jars if one touched any contaminant. You might have overheard a Jewish wife saying, "Honey, get me stoneware this year, I'm tired of replacing clay pots. I mean, they are so last century!"

Jesus instructs the servants to fill the stone vessels with water—about 20-30 gallons each! Imagine them hauling 120-180 gallons of water from the well. They filled them right to the rim.[12] Instantly, the water changed to the purest and best wine (not best because of high alcohol content but richest flavor). From that which could only rinse the outside of the body Jesus made that which would satisfy the inside.

Jesus had the servants ladle some of the beverage into a cup and bring it to the master of ceremonies.[13] Imagine being that servant carrying a cup of water to the wedding organizer. Talk about feeling like a fool. But servants do what they are told anyway.

When this wedding organizer tasted it, his eyebrows jumped. He calls over the groom. "Where did you get this? That is the best ever. Usually people serve the store brand a few days

---

[10] John 2:6, LITV.

[11] See also Mark 7:2-5.

[12] John 2:7, LITV.

[13] See John 2:8-9.

into the wedding, but you are closing out this event with the best in the house!"[14]

Don't miss the spiritual meaning here.

As a Groom-to-be, Jesus saved face for the soon-to-be-embarrassed bridegroom. He prevented a nice girl from becoming a Bride-zilla.[15] He gave us a glimpse of what His wedding feast will be like—saving the best for last. We will talk more about that wedding later, much later.

This was the first sign Jesus did.[16] A sign points to something greater than itself. The point of the story was not to show us that we don't have to worry about planning ahead at weddings, of course. This miracle points to Jesus.

What signs do we see here?

- Fullness. Jesus filled the empty vessels to the brim.
- Abundance. Over a hundred gallons of wedding punch! That's insane! But in the Kingdom there is always too much.
- From dead to living. He changed what was inside. A fermented beverage has living qualities to it.

Signs are more than just for humans. This against-the-laws-of-nature event served notice to the kingdom of darkness that everything was about to change. Those devoted to purity would soon be pouring forth with what is powerful.

The disciples did not take part in this miracle, but they didn't miss it either. They were following, remember. They didn't miss the cagey exchange between Jesus and Mary. They observed Him instructing the servants to get more water when they needed wine instead. They saw Him send the servants to make

---

[14] See John 2:10.

[15] An angry bride who becomes a rage monster like the legendary Godzilla.

[16] See John 2:11.

fools of themselves. They saw the look on the master of ceremonies' face when he tasted the new wine.

Only the disciples saw what happened, but they could have missed it. Andrew could have gotten distracted talking to the bride's cute cousin. John could have spent too much time at the punch bowl and been the reason it was empty.

Instead, in normal experiences and daily life, they were watching Jesus at work. Are you? This is part of your training.

Something happened inside His followers. This sign "revealed His glory, and His disciples believed into Him."[17] This is the step beyond just seeing Jesus. A central shift occurred.

Deep in their hearts a switch flipped. This miracle in front of them penetrated deeper than logic circuits in their brains. He hit the core, shaking the impulse-and-response center and penetrating their subconscious mind.

They would never look at physical matter the same way again. The Kingdom from above can manipulate matter in this world below. Everything life had taught them about how things worked suddenly shifted.

Jesus had done something impossible according to normal human explanation. Seeing that miracle moved their trust from experience to Jesus. He could do anything.

To "believe into" Jesus means He becomes the center of your universe. None of your experiences can be trusted now. He can transform the very elements of nature, heal a broken heart, and give purpose to a discarded life.

We begin to do everything with Jesus in view. Our goals, values, friendships, and expectations all change when He becomes the basis of our existence. Your total trust and dependence on Jesus might come through a series of subtle, slow

---

[17] John 2:11, LITV.

14

changes. It could be dramatic, sweeping changes all at once like a wedding crisis (or marriage crisis).

What you must do is respond as the servants. He will speak into your world. Even if it does not make sense, do it.

Sure, this event impressed the disciples, but it was not really their own crisis. So why would it trigger them to throw their whole weight on Jesus? The disciples saw that Jesus had something better than humanity's best. He superseded the traditions like the stone containers and all other attempts at self-cleansing.

Belief is not emotion. True faith resets your value system to the core. It happens in your head and in your spirit. You base every decision, choice, and emotion on Jesus rather than self.

What drives the normal mind? Fear, for one. When you have been reset by Jesus, there is no need to fear threats, poverty, or the unknown. Fear gives way to a more powerful trigger: faith. He also trades love for anger, hope for shame.

They did not just believe the story about Jesus, as many Christians promote today. Something deep happened when they saw the impossible happen with just a whisper. As we move forward, we will learn more of what it means to believe.

Humans think they can be okay by behaving okay. Jesus, however, did a transforming work in a way no one can see. They only saw the results of it; no one knew what had happened but those on the "inside." So, deep within, He is changing you.

This miracle sign shows us:

- Jesus will fill empty vessels (that's us)
- with the best (that's Himself), which
- He has saved for the end of earth's party (that's now).

The Jewish disciples saw something else we might miss: Moses being replaced by Jesus. Seeing Jesus as greater than their religion, their faith shifted toward Him.

Jesus did ministry in front of His disciples in real life, not a classroom lecture. Training them included vocal instruction, but it was as much or more about "doing" than just "talking." He is active in your life if you are watching. Don't get distracted by the party around you or overwhelmed at the problems—look and see what He is doing behind the scenes for you.

WHO GETS THE HOUSE?

I MAGINE WHAT SOME of the disciples were thinking after they left the wedding. "If He can change the nature of water, what else can He do?" As they trudged the dusty road to Capernaum, they thought it over.

The more you learn about Jesus, the more certain things just click into place in your mind and heart. You get new information and you see Him better. Those insights reshape how you pray and how you think about life.

Capernaum, "Village of Nahum," likely referred to the prophet Nahum from hundreds of years prior. It also means "Village of comfort." In Capernaum, Jesus would do His greatest miracles.[18] That city became His base of operations while in Galilee.

Like other rabbis, Jesus had selected quality persons he wanted to disciple. Soon, He would be asking them for a long-term commitment. After a short period of observing him, if they decided to follow the rabbi, they would learn his ways and become like him. It was like a person-sized franchise. They

---

[18] See Luke 4:23 and Matthew 11:23.

would later teach others by word and action the same way their rabbi taught them.

Jesus took His disciples with Him to His own house. He also brought along His mother and brothers.[19] The absence of Joseph's name in the story indicates that Mary's husband had already passed away by this time. Being Mary's oldest son, Jesus would have become their caretaker and provider. Jesus's brothers lived with Him, but did not follow Him. Yet.

After a short time, Jesus headed south again to Jerusalem. His disciples followed, but his family members stayed there in Capernaum. Staying comfortable would not transform them into what Jesus had designed them to be. True growth will happen beyond the village of comfort.

It was early spring when He led those followers to the most publicized feast in Judaism, Passover.[20] This is the first record of His visiting Jerusalem after entering into His official commission as Messiah, the undercover King.

Entering the Temple grounds, Jesus encountered a market of sheep, goats, and bulls. The smell of the organic fertilizer made the courtyard into a stockyard instead of a prayer meeting. The mooing, bleating, and baaing made it feel like a petting zoo. Though it doesn't sound appetizing, if you were serious about your faith, you would have been eating something from this menu.

Many visitors to the Temple would offer an animal sacrifice. At Passover, every family was to offer a lamb. So, it is not a shock to Jesus to see so many sheep, doves, and other animals.[21] The shock comes at the realization that those who were entrusted with leading the people were using worship as a moneymaker.

---

[19] See John 2;12.

[20] See John 2:13.

[21] See John 2:14.

The Temple elite, including Sadducees, Sanhedrin, and especially the high priest, became so focused on the financial transactions at hand that they became blinded to the God they were supposed to be worshiping. Something similar happens to many Christian institutions today.

Just as we would find it odd for someone to be sitting on a pew munching on a Chik-Fil-A sandwich, so Jesus saw it odd for the place of worship to be all about consumerism. Additionally, the foreign exchange tables were set up to convert other nations' money into the Temple shekel and its derivatives. The unaccountable leadership was "making bank" from this operation.

The Temple of that day had a "no conceal and carry" policy. A sign on the Temple grounds said no weapons were allowed. The Sicarii (sik-AR-ee) were Jewish assassins who used daggers to target high profile people in the large crowds. Perhaps because a man could not carry a whip onto the Temple grounds, Jesus stopped and made one on the spot.

Even in anger for the right cause, pausing to do something constructive (braiding a whip from cords) could help keep us from being reckless in our wrath. It does not say that Jesus hit the market makers, but He did drive them out with their animals. He also dumped out all the money of the currency traders.[22]

Once the tables had turned, Jesus spoke to those merchants who were left—apparently just the bird keepers—and to all the other worshippers who might overhear. "Get these things out of here!"[23]

All religious traditions tend toward corruption with time. The Temple was the religious institute designed by God, but selfish humans had infiltrated it. We need Jesus to snap us out of our comfort zone so we see things correctly.

---

[22] See John 2:15.
[23] Not an exact quote of John 2:16.

What was the reset for these hardened traditionalists? Jesus is the Temple, God's house. Remember, the Gospel of John already introduced the idea that the "Word" tabernacled in flesh,[24] and Jesus hinted to Nathanael that He was the House of God that Jacob described.[25]

Unfortunately, many people make their lives a "house of merchandise" by living for personal gain rather than His. Do you live to make money? Are you here for what profit you can get from life? Or are you looking to give back, to help others find the Lord?

Some church buildings today might only be "houses of merchandise." Not only do they have carefully crafted business models for profitability, they lack what they were intended for: a place to meet with the Lord. Some mega-churches have franchises, also called satellite churches, on campuses all over the map.

A big-box church put a satellite location in our city. Members would come to view the founding "guru" preacher on the big screen each Sunday morning. Of course, the building had all the carefully crafted banners, programs, and other attractants for the typical evangelical consumer of today. No wonder the mega-pastor could afford a personal helicopter. Someone who attended there told me he would land in the parking lot to wow the congregation with an in-the-flesh, surprise appearance.

Like Burger King or McDonald's, these kinds of churches have popped up in every major community, proudly displaying their brands and logos. And we should be happy about this. After all, more people are now able to kill sheep and leave their money on campus for the "house of the Lord."

---

[24] See John 1:14.

[25] See John 1:51 with Genesis 28:12-19. The second chapter of John will reveal more about Jesus as the Temple in a moment. Today, true believers are the Temple of God on earth, the place on earth where His presence dwells (I Corinthians 3:16-17; 6:19).

Would Jesus approve? What does Jesus think of churches today? Would He take a whip to the board members and businessmen running the show? Jesus did not start a chain of Temple franchises. Instead, we should buy into "The Jesus Franchise." We, as individuals, become what He is.

The disciples saw Jesus cracking a whip in the Temple. He called out to the people to not live for money. Seeing this, His followers remembered a Scripture about being consumed with zeal for God's house.[26] Jesus's passion was an example for them.

Are you driven by a desire to get back to heart-felt relationship with the Lord? Or are you being sucked down the drain of religious professionalism? True followers of Jesus adopt this "I don't care what others think of me" fanaticism for the Kingdom. We all should.

Notice the knowledge these disciples had of the Bible: "His disciples remembered that it was written..."[27] Not every disciple starts out here. Jesus had a short work to do and that might be part of the reason He began with disciples who already knew the Holy Writings. His first disciples could not have seen Jesus correctly if they had not known how this Bible passage applied to Him.

Those who only know a little about the Bible will start building their knowledge of the Scriptures, if they are true trainees of our Rabbi. To see Jesus fully, you must know His Book.

My goal in these writings it to help you have an in-depth awareness of the Holy Scriptures regarding Jesus. That is also why I offer you the *Handbook for Your Factory Reset* as well.[28]

---

[26] See John 2:17 with Psalm 69:9.

[27] John 2:17, LITV.

[28] You can download the Handbook for free and print it or buy the paperback version. Go to Jesusin2020.com for more details.

That volume will help guide you through the same Scriptures we are discussing in this book.

A man sits on his spine on an overstuffed couch with a thin dusting from cheese curls over his T-shirt. He licks the orange smudges off the ends of his fingers while watching the TV screen. Meanwhile a man sits in a stadium wearing a foam hat cut in the shape of a cheese wedge in 10 degree weather, cheering for the same team. On the field, another man takes a brain-shaking blow as three other players tackle him on the 20-yard line.

You see the different levels of dedication there. Which one are you? Are you a watcher of Jesus or are you eaten up with the cause?

Our impulsive choices come from deep in the midbrain. You cannot talk to that part of the body; you cannot educate it into action. It was imprinted early in life. Jesus was born with a drive for the things from above.

What drives you? What is your passion? Food? Styles? Career?

Some people are passionate about their church building. That is not evil. However, we should not mistake a house of worship for the House of God. Jesus will make the distinction clearer for us in our next chapter.

The disciples were amazed at the miracle power they saw in Cana and that confirmed their hopes about Jesus. Now they see the passion He has for the cause. They will follow this Leader and develop that same red-hot desire.

RAZE THE TEMPLE

THE ROOM IS QUIET and dark. Intentionally, no noise or bright lights dominate the scene. Instrumental music plays softly in the background. After a few tense minutes, a newborn baby rises slowly to the water's surface. This is gentle birth, a water birth in a non-frightening room.

Instead of opening his mouth and screaming, the baby opens his eyes. Quickly adjusting to the dimly lit room, this non-traumatized baby has a rare opportunity in the civilized world: to experience birth without unnecessary drama.

He blinks and refocuses his widely dilated pupils. These fully functional eyes work perfectly from day one. However, perfectly formed as they are, they will have to develop and strengthen to focus better and further in a room.

Early on, certain colors and tones will catch his eye quickest. Over weeks and months, he will learn to look at more than just twinkling lights, gliding mobiles, and shiny objects. He will soon look fully into the eyes of his parents. He will recognize who is holding him and learn to communicate with his eyes and voice.

Sight does not begin with comprehension. It begins with seeing. Yes, immediately the light can enter the lens, go through the retina, and land on the rod-and-cone nerves at the back of the eyeball. The optic nerve must be functioning for the eyes to see. The brain has to flip the upside down image and begin to learn what all those objects and motions mean.

When a new disciple begins glimpsing Jesus, they will not understand. Spiritual eyes need time to focus and register what they see. One then learns how to respond to all that data. In the coming stories of the Lord's life, we will see that infant faith in others and how to develop it.

Jesus had just crashed the foreign exchange market, shocking the powerful leaders at the Temple. They demanded, "What sign do You show to us, since You do these things?"[29] Since the unbelieving cannot see spiritually, their immature eyes look for physical proof. They have not developed "facial recognition" of the Master.

When the unseeing people come along telling Jesus what they want to see, He gives them a message that is way out of focus for them: "Destroy this sanctuary, and in three days I will raise it up."[30] They don't get it. The whole image looks fuzzy to them. Destroy their Temple? Rebuild in 3 days?

The Jewish leaders glared at Him, reminding him that their beloved sanctuary (holy place, temple) had been under construction for 46 years.[31] They knew it would take more than 3 days to rebuild their Temple. I hear them ask, "Do we look stupid or something?" Well...

Unbelievers are unbelievers because they cannot see or comprehend. Like eyes sending a signal that the brain cannot yet recognize, whatever they glimpse of Him never gets mapped on

---

[29] John 2:18, LITV.

[30] John 2:19, LITV.

[31] See John 2:20.

their unspiritual mind. In the unseen realm, things are just as real and create just as vivid an impression as those things in the seen realm. However, spiritual blindness is a personal choice, not a deformity.

The disciples, spiritual babies who could see Jesus, did not comprehend this statement about rebuilding the Temple either. They saw but did not perceive. Yes, their spiritual minds shifted when they saw Jesus work the miracle in Cana. They believe. Their focus developed even more when they saw His zeal in the Temple.

Although they saw clearly as He said that "three days" statement, their understanding lagged behind. Three years later, their minds will connect what happened in the tomb with what He said then.[32] Jesus was talking about His death and resurrection—no one could see that yet. That vision was so far out of range for these who did see Jesus that it never developed in their comprehension until after He rose again.

Jesus was not talking about the building Herod was paying to remodel. John wrote that story long after His eyes began clearly seeing Jesus. In hindsight, he let us in on a little tip: "He spoke about the sanctuary [temple] of His body."[33] The body of Jesus is the true house of God!

Are you seeing Jesus yet finding yourself perplexed? Are you stretching to understand at times? Good! Like a baby developing mind maps, you will comprehend the more you look. Do not give up. The more you see in the Spirit, the more meaning it will all have later.

A three-year-old's eyeballs have not developed much more than what they were at 3 months. The three-year-old's comprehension however is much better because he or she has been learning what all those visible objects mean. Keep looking

---

[32] See John 2:22.
[33] See John 2:21.

into the Kingdom even when you do not understand; you're mapping out your understanding.

Sometimes a person sees a spiritual truth and makes a snap response when they do not have all the info. You cannot rush your growth—think of your faith as being more about relationship with Jesus than a quest for information. You may have begun this because you wanted to know everything you could about the Lord. Really what you wanted was to know Him as a person.

Will you join the "show us a sign" crowd? Those religious people at the Temple wanted to see something, but not what Jesus wanted to show them. They wanted shock and awe.

The enemy in the last days works lying signs and wonders. If you do not continually imprint yourself with the true Jesus of Scripture, you will be deceived. If miracles and amazing tricks light your wick, then you might be easily deceived. True faith is not about shivers up your spine or warm fuzzy feelings.

Jesus did not come to show off power (as Satan does) but to show Himself. True works of God help us see Him better. Many "Christian" movements have gone off the rails chasing after amazing people who were not helping them see Jesus.

Others can only see their comfort zones. Jesus brought His disciples out of the "village of comfort" (Capernaum). Many people do not want to leave their comfortable traditions and opinions. Most are manmade or misapplied behaviors that seem self-validating, but have no biblical basis.

What if you put aside all your rituals about prayer, your routine that you call worship, or your special "do's and don'ts" and just saw Jesus? Perhaps many things you do will remain. Perhaps He will give new meaning to old actions.

Jesus shocked His listeners that day. Tearing down the Temple meant destroying tons of gold, beautiful marble walls, and intricately woven tapestries. The building stood over sixty feet tall!

What amazing shrines might He call from your life so He can rebuild it after His design? Remember, He challenged them to tear it down: "Destroy this sanctuary."[34] They couldn't imagine a total reset of all they had ever known. What rut, ritual, and comfortable behavior will you bring Him so He can remake you in His glory?

Have you ever taken a picture when your finger was in front of the camera lens? I don't like to see my finger in the frame. I must get myself out of the picture. My goals, dreams, and self-focus all must die so He can be raised up in me!

The Temple is Jesus's body. And yours. He is not just wanting to tear down little parts of your life but is calling you to submit your whole self for demolition. We must get ourselves out of the picture.

What happened to that Temple they defended so religiously? They kept remodeling it for 30 more years. Then it was smashed about a decade after that. That building did not come back after three days. Jesus did.

This is the Maker's reset. Everything human must be crushed. Jesus rises up in us.

---

[34] John 2:19, LITV.

UPGRADE OR NAH?

JESUS BEGAN MIRACLES at the wedding, and then He did more in Jerusalem, after He cleaned the House, of course. Now, like the disciples did at first, "many believed into His name, seeing the miracles which He did."[35] Those who paid attention, some of the common people, knew something big was happening. Though they did not know what Jesus was all about, they opened their eyes enough to see that He had more than their religious powerbrokers had.

Jesus answered the request for signs with one that stumped them: razing the Temple. Those star-struck fans ran after Jesus because of the supernatural events. They switched loyalties because of what they saw with their natural eyes. Our five senses do not connect with the Spirit.

People have done this countless times. Dramatic things happen and huge flocks of people show up to see and someone calls it "revival!" Jesus did not get excited about the popularity. Their belief in Him was not the same as a true reset. It was more like installing a new app, even putting it on their home screen.

---

[35] John 2:23, LITV. The same word for "sign" (*sēmeion*) in verse 18 is the same for "miracle" in 23.

Quick conversions do not hold the value costly conversions do. These people had not changed much but their T-shirt, so to speak. Their label now read "Jesus of Nazareth" instead of "Pharisee Club" or something similar.

Many "Christians" cling to some tribe or spiritual celebrity. Others chase signs. They go from one religious attraction center to another, following one charming TV personality and then another. They are chasing a wow-effect and will leave the true Jesus easily if something more dazzling comes along.

Though some in this crowd believed in Jesus, He did not believe in them.[36] Jesus did not commit to, believe in, or put His trust in the wow crowd.[37] Why? Because they were the fly-by-night crowd. They would run off and chase the next shiny thing.

Jesus is not looking for hero-worshipers but servant-followers. This is not just about believing in Jesus but believing with the right motive. We will see in a few chapters what true belief looks like.

Jesus knows that humans are untrustworthy. He can see right through us: "He had no need that anyone should witness concerning man, for He knew what was in man."[38] Knowing this, when a distinguished gentleman approached Him, Jesus could see right through him: "But there was a man from the Pharisees, Nicodemus his name, a ruler of the Jews."[39] Jesus knows all that is in humans and here comes a human now, named Nick.

Nicodemus might have been like a mega-church pastor today. He was a ruler of the Jews. This means he may have led

---

[36] See John 2:24.

[37] From Greek *pisteuo*. This word is the same in John 2:23 for their "believing" in Him and in 2:24 where He said He did not "commit Himself to them."

[38] John 2:24, LITV.

[39] John 3:1, LITV.

the synagogue in Jerusalem. He was likely also a member of the Sanhedrin, the strongest governmental arm of Israel at the time, similar to a senate or congress today. As either pastor or politician, his position as a leading Pharisee in Jerusalem made him a man of wide influence.

Pharisees wore tassels on their clothing so they would think about the writings of Torah[40] all the time. They took literally the part about God's commands being tied to the forehead and hand. Of course, those who did this became proud about how devoted they were. What began as a revival of prayer, fasting, and holy living became a tradition for the sake of the tradition, with little true relationship with God.

We see Nick say, "Rabbi, we know that You have come as a teacher from God. For no one is able to do these miraculous signs which You do, except God be with Him."[41] Nick was one of those who saw the signs and believed in Jesus. He was a man, a religious man, a leader man. Jesus knew what was in a man and did not believe in him.

In the darkness, Nick saw Jesus only dimly. He couldn't see clearly yet, but he knew something important was happening. By contrast, John the Baptizer saw Jesus clearly and came to bear witness of the Light.[42] John the writer took care to record those details. The preacher in the wilderness was in the light; the preacher in Jerusalem was in the dark.

Nicodemus saw Jesus as teacher. He saw signs. He saw God was with Him.

Like the baby with new eyes that see but do not comprehend, Nick was blinking into the darkness, gazing at the Light. Nick saw power but he did not see Kingdom. He saw teacher, but he did not see King. Baby sight must grow in focus

---

[40] The teachings written by Moses.

[41] John 3:2, LITV.

[42] See John 1:6-8.

and comprehension. At least Nick knew he was looking at something great even if he didn't understand what, yet.

Think back to that baby who is beginning to comprehend. He can see his favorite ball, but that does not mean he can show us the way to the mall. Just because a child can recognize the food court does not mean she knows how to get you to Dillard's or Trade Home Shoes. Following people who do not see Jesus clearly is a huge risk. Like Nick, many religious leaders today claim Jesus, but they must come to see Him clearly, not in the dark.

Jesus will now deepen Nick's field of vision. "If one is not generated from above, he is not able to see the kingdom of God."[43] The popular way of translating this verse is more like: "unless one is born again."[44] A person must be born to see.

The phrase "born again" comes to us from people who could not see Jesus very well. What I am about to say might upset you. I hope it *re*sets you.

Modern "can't see Jesus" types of Christian leaders popularized the use of the phrase "born again." Many good people use this phrase as a core aspect of what they believe it means to be a Christian. Yet they are blinded to what the phrase really means.

So was Nick.

When Jesus mentions being born, Nick squints, raises his eyebrows, and then tries to comprehend. "So, you're saying I have to go back inside my mother's womb and be born a second time?"[45] But Jesus did not say "born a second time" or even "born again."

---

43 John 3:3, LITV.
44 John 3:3, NKJV.
45 See John 3:34.

It only sounded like He did.

The phrase "born again" should not be in your Bible. There it is. That impulse to close this book.

I must be crazy. Every Christian believes you must be born again. Right?

The phrase "born again" is in English versions because the Bible translators were probably as blind to Truth as Nicodemus was. They could not see Jesus well enough to translate this statement about what it takes to see the Kingdom. That word could have been translated either as "again" or "from above."[46] In fact, a few paragraphs later Jesus says He is the One "from above."[47]

Nick, the man who cannot see Jesus, thought He said, "born a second time." It would be impossible to be born a second time (or "again") because that means repeating the same thing. We don't need a reinstall of the same software. We don't need a do-over of human birth but a birth from above—where Jesus is from. When we understand this "from above" expression, the rest of what Jesus says makes sense.

Modern Christianity has interpreted Jesus's words through Nick's filter rather than through Jesus's own explanation. We will get to that in the next chapter. Jesus comes "from above" and this is different than being from the earth. We know Jesus is the Lord "from heaven." Those who are not born from heaven will not see the Kingdom. Some believe like Nick; others are born from above.

---

[46] This Greek word is *anothen*. It refers to something from above, from a higher place, or something anew and thus "over again." It is translated as "top" in Matthew 27:51 and Mark 15:38; "first" or "beginning" in Luke 1:3 and Acts 26:5; "above" in John 3:31; 19:11, 23 and James 1:17; 3:15, 17. It is handled as a "again" or "anew" in Galatians 4:9.

[47] See John 3:31.

Truth belief is not accepting information as true. When you believe something, it affects your impulses and defaults. This factory reset flips your life into a mode drastically different than your old motivations and reflexes. When you trust Jesus to the core, your subconscious decisions and desires change.

Imagine you visit a popular denominational church and ask one of the volunteers, "How can I be born again?" Typically, an evangelical person would tell you that you must believe on Jesus. However, Jesus was talking to a man who believed in Him and still told him he must be born from above.

Being born from above is not to just believe in Jesus. You will see this conclusively in the next chapter. Like Pastor Nick, many people follow a religious tradition and have no understanding. They are not bad people, they are just infants who do not comprehend what they see.

The prevailing Christian thought system today has been built on misunderstanding. Should it be kicked over and chased out with a whip?

BORN FROM ABOVE

ROYAL FOOD TURNS commoners into royalty. Can you believe that? Just eating the right thing could put an unlikely one in authority!

I'm talking about honeybees.

Nothing you eat as a human will make you a king or queen. Nothing you do in your flesh can make you divine. However, a normal worker honeybee will become queen of the colony if she is fed the right diet.

Yes, the caretaker bees feed her royal jelly, causing her to develop in special ways the other larvae don't. The catch is that although anyone could be royal, they must be fed correctly in infancy. This is a spiritual truth.

You could have been royal. You could rule and reign in life. However, after your birth, your caretakers only could give you earthly food.

If a common bee could become queen by being fed royal jelly after birth, you and I have a chance at nobility if we start over. Being born from above gives us a chance at becoming a higher life form, something that will outlast this world. By changing what we feed on, we will develop correctly this time.

Would you commit to feast only an royal food for the next 40 days? Jesus went into the wilderness and ate nothing but what proceeded from the mouth of God. Rather than read novels, watch TV shows, or gorge yourself on gaming, put your focus on Jesus, His Book, and feasting only on what comes from above.

In the first book in this series, we talked a lot about seeing Jesus. Now, Jesus tells us about seeing the Kingdom. A person cannot see it unless he or she has been born from above. Are you looking through the eyes of royalty? Or do you come to the Kingdom as a peasant?

Birth is a dramatic thing. A baby cannot see the world we live in until he or she is out of the womb. You and I cannot see the Kingdom until our new birth.

Have you noticed how few Christians talk about the Kingdom of God? I'm stunned at how many do not see the Kingdom. I look back and wonder how I missed it for so many years. Yes, I used the words "Kingdom of God" back then but did not see it.

Most believers see their church. They see their denomination/organization, if they are in one. Still, many couldn't define the Kingdom of God to save their souls.

A kingdom is a realm governed by laws established by the king. It has a military force, economic system, unique climate, and defined territory. God's Kingdom has all that and more. We will look at the Kingdom details in a later book.

Like nations on earth, to belong to the Kingdom of God, you need proper citizenship.[48] Unlike an earthly government,

---

[48] See also Matthew 22:11-14.

you cannot do any paperwork to immigrate to this Kingdom. You have to be born there; no exceptions.

Many people think that if they do the right things, they will be granted citizenship in the Kingdom above. That is like a dog doing the right things to become a human. I'm sure you've seen the humanized dog before, maybe you own one:

- It wears a sweater.
- It sleeps in its master's bed.
- Its bowl gets washed in the dishwasher.
- It likes air conditioning.

However, no matter how much she learns to speak, sit up, or watch cat videos, that doggie will never be human. It cannot behave human enough to leave the dog kingdom and join the human kingdom. That would take a miracle.

Likewise, no one will behave heavenly enough to leave the kingdom of earth. You only become human by being born into the human kingdom. All other creatures are stuck in the realms of their gene pool. Likewise, you only become Jesus by being born from above.

The kingdoms of earth operate by spite, hate, lust, and greed. The Kingdom from above functions by sacrifice, sharing, giving, suffering, loving, and restoring. God's Kingdom transcends our politics and problems of life. To be reset into the heavenly Kingdom, pay close attention to the words of the first Citizen and King of that realm from above.

Jesus speaks truth. He began His Kingdom statements with "Truly, truly,"[49] or "Most assuredly."[50] His truth confronted false beliefs. Nick not only had the wrong idea about spiritual

---

[49] In John 3:3, 5, LITV.

[50] In John 3:3, 5, NKJV. Two words repeated like this form a superlative, in the original. Literally, He said, "Amen, amen."

things but was a teacher within the Pharisee tradition which was full of wrong notions.

There's no telling what Nick expected to hear when he went to visit Jesus. He thought Jesus was a specially empowered prophet. It would have been to his best advantage to have a close connection with Him.

Jesus shifted the conversation from a business card swap session to a focus on the Kingdom of God. First, He said one cannot see it until they are God-born. This insight blew Nicodemus's mind.

Next, Jesus clarified that one cannot enter the Kingdom until they are born from above. Seeing Jesus is not the same as entering the Kingdom. One cannot enter the Kingdom of God if that "one is not generated out of water and Spirit."[51]

To be "generated" from above is to be "born of water and Spirit."[52] All the instances referring to water in John chapter one were in reference to John baptizing/immersing converts in the river.[53] All of Jesus's disciples had been baptized[54] and later in John chapter three we see them help baptize others. Water immersion surrounds this conversation.

The complement to John's immersion was Jesus's. John came to immerse in water; Jesus came to immerse with Spirit. In no uncertain terms, Jesus shows that these are not symbolic rituals but truly, truly a transformative experience: immersion of water and Spirit. We already saw that plunging into the water at the hands of John brought cleansing from sin.

---

[51] John 3:5, LITV.

[52] John 3:5, NKJV.

[53] See John 1:26, 31, 33.

[54] In Acts 1:22, Peter identified the apostles with those who were first baptized by John.

When a repentant person went under the water, they came back up with a new identity as a disciple of John.[55] Likewise, when a person becomes immersed in the Spirit, they become a new individual—a disciple of Jesus. There is more to this, but watch what Jesus is saying to Nick.

Nicodemus had already rejected John's baptism, being a Pharisee who did not think he needed cleansing from someone else. Today, you will also hear people say, "It's just me and God. I don't need anyone else." Nick could not enter the Kingdom if he was not born of water (introduced by John) and Spirit (by Jesus).

Nick was one of those who believed in Jesus.[56] His confidence in Jesus was not enough. Jesus had no confidence in him unless he would be born from above.

What about all the people today who say they have trusted in Jesus? Have they had the factory reset? Or did they just install a "Jesus app" into their lives?

The Lord Jesus is not something we add to our already pretty-good lives. He is our total transformation into something new. Not just an update but a fresh install of a whole new operating system.

As humans, we come from beneath. God formed Adam out of dirt. Though Adam and Eve reflect the image of the Eternal One, they came from the substance of that which decays rather than endures. When human bodies die, they return to the earth they came from.

Jesus's conception came from above. When He died, He returned to His point of origin, so to speak—the heavenly realm.

---

[55] There was more to that baptism. It was immersion as a person living in expectancy of the coming of the King. However, for onlookers, these new believers were baptized as followers of John.

[56] See John 2:23.

So also, those who are born from above with Jesus will go where He is when they die:

> "The first man was of the earth, made of dust; the second Man is the Lord from heaven. As was the man of dust, so also are those who are made of dust; and as is the heavenly Man, so also are those who are heavenly. And as we have borne the image of the man of dust, we shall also bear the image of the heavenly Man."[57]

See how this is a transforming process? We are talking about something bigger than just a change of thinking but a substantial change of identity.

Remember how we talked about the phrase "born again" that is so common in Christian language? Many modern believers have redefined the phrase "born again" to describe the kind of uncommitted belief Jesus would not commit Himself to ("Just say this prayer with me and you will be born again"). To believe such a thing, they have to make John 3:5 mean nothing.

Jesus said, "Most assuredly, I say to you, unless one is born of water and the Spirit, he cannot enter the kingdom of God."[58] So, many religious people take Jesus's "most assuredly" and try to reassure us He did not mean what He said. They say you don't have to be born of water and that being born of the Spirit is the same as believing.

What? Why try to change what He said? It all goes back to being spiritually blinded. Rather than remove the cataracts or stained glass, they just try to define Him by what they think they see.

Religious lenses cause some of those pop theologians to say that "born of water" must mean being born of a woman. Though a womb contains amniotic fluid, that does not make it a

---

57 I Corinthians 15:47-49, NKJV.
58 John 3:5, NKJV.

water birth. This statement about being "born of water"[59] comes in the context of passages where the word "water" refers to the pivotal act of water immersion.[60] We should not overlook the backstory behind this encounter.

No Jewish statement ever referred to natural birth as "born of water." Rather, proselytes into Judaism had to be washed for cleansing and this was referred to as "born of water" at times.[61] Keep in mind also that the Pharisees rejected John's baptism, and Nick is one of the Pharisees from Jerusalem.[62]

Jews considered themselves specially born. They were the special race with the DNA of Abraham, which they believed entitled them to God's favor. Jesus told Nick that his birth into Judaism meant nothing. He must have another birth, from above.

You can imagine Nicodemus was dumbfounded. He'd never had another Jew tell him that his Jewishness was nothing. Imagine someone saying a pastor of a thriving and successful church was outside God's realm. Those are fighting words.

John had told the Pharisees that God could perform a "factory reset" on rocks to make children of Abraham if He wanted.[63] Abraham's true offspring do not share ol' Abe's bloodline but his total dependence on God.[64] John explained that He would immerse with water, bringing a moral reset to the lives

---

[59] John 3:5, NKJV.

[60] The preceding references to water washing include John 1:26, 31, 33.

[61] See Craig Keener, *John*, Vol. 1.

[62] See John 1:24-25 and more specifically Luke 7:30. In Matthew 3:7-12, John refused to immerse Pharisees in water because they refused to have a factory reset.

[63] See Matthew 3:9 or Luke 3:8.

[64] See Galatians 3:26-29.

of those turning from sin. He further explained that Jesus would immerse with the Spirit, completing the factory reset.[65]

The Gospel of John prepared us for this night-time revelation with Nick. John said, "The One sending me to baptize in water, that One said to me, 'On whomever you see the Spirit coming down and abiding on Him, this is the One baptizing in the Holy Spirit.'"[66] Notice the connection again between water and Spirit immersion? Jesus's conversation with Nick continues that emphasis.

Also, the phrase "born from above" is an equal expression to being "born of water and Spirit."[67] The second phrase expands and explains how the first one occurs. Nicodemus asked, "How can I be born again?" Jesus explained: "be born of water and Spirit."

I realize some people might hate me for emphasizing this point because there are so many "born again" ministries, songs, and book titles. Another common phrase from this conversation is "born a second time" or "second birth." Notice who said that though: Nick at night. The man in the dark. The religious leader who did not see.

So why does everyone quote the man who didn't get it instead of the Man who gives it? We looked in the last chapter at how the phrase "born from above" could mean two different things: a birth on top of a birth (happening a second time) or a birth from the top (coming from a higher place).[68] Nicodemus

---

[65] See John 1:33 as well as Matthew 3:11-12 or Luke 3:16.

[66] John 1:33, LITV, single quotes added for clarity.

[67] John 3:3, 5, NKJV.

[68] Of course, I am being extreme in my emphasis here to drive home the idea of being "born from above." It is not evil to use the expression "born again" as long as we know what it represents. To help shift our thinking from dead ruts, we need to change the words we use. Jesus and other writers in Scripture invented new words or gave old words new meaning in order to help listeners understand the new concepts.

did not understand, so he asked a clarifying question. Let's not quote the confused man's question but the answer of the One from above!

Jesus did not intend for us to enter our mother's wombs again. He did not intend for us to be born a second time of the flesh. This is not about improving what we already have, but replacing it.

Something born of the flesh (from beneath) is just flesh.[69] Jesus explained: "That having been generated out of the flesh is flesh, and that having been generated out of the Spirit is spirit."[70] No matter how many times you restart your phone, it still has the same operating system. That which comes from above—the Spirit—will birth us in a new way. Jesus was literally generated from above, being conceived of the Holy Spirit.[71]

Those reset from above have defaults of love, faith, and joy. When the Spirit flips that switch in your mind and soul, you will handle decisions differently. When the Spirit resets your will and emotions, you will respond and react to life positively rather than negatively.

Unfortunately, many people claim to have been filled with the Spirit, but have not had a massive shift in their life. I don't doubt their sensational experience. However, having an amazing encounter with Jesus should continue to reset everything about us.

A new operating system on your phone requires you to reinstall all the apps again. The new software changes the way your device interacts with other applications. So, the Spirit dwelling in us, changes how we handle money, free time, entertainment, and friendships.

---

[69] Jesus later uses this distinction in John 8:23: "You are from below; I am from above. You are from this world; I am not from this world." LITV.

[70] John 3:6, LITV.

[71] See Matthew 1:20.

John's Gospel connects the idea of water and washing a few times, both with John's ministry and later when Jesus sent a blind man to wash his blindness from his eyes. The audience who first received the Gospel of John understood God's command to be washed in water for the cleansing of sin and would have seen "born of water" to indicate that. A supernatural thing happens when a person obeys Jesus's plan of water baptism—this "reset" washes away sin.

To be from above, we must also be born in the Spirit. Spirit immersion causes something new to come alive within you. I have watched true conversion flip a switch in people's minds, resetting their default from fear to faith, from hate to love. You choose to live from that new power.

Those from Adam (all humans) came from beneath—the earth. Those from above, as is Jesus Christ, take on an eternal identity. The new birth resets that part inside that lives forever.

Those generated of earth will return to it when they die. Those generated by heaven will go to it when they die. There is no middle place.

A genetic child of someone carries their DNA. This is also true in spiritual birth. DNA is a code, a message, a spiritual transfer. True children of God were born "not of blood, nor of the will of the flesh, nor of the will of man, but were born of God."[72] Talk about an extreme makeover.

The Kingdom of God does not follow human ability, emotions, or methods. Like DNA, we find this code woven tightly into the Gospels. That is why we will take a while to unzip it all (I have a few more books coming to help us unpack everything in the Gospels). Let yourself be changed day by day into the image of Christ.

---

[72] John 1:13, LITV.

You will know

BIRTH BEGINS LIFE. Unfortunately many who parrot the phrase "born again" also treat salvation as an ending rather than a beginning. They say, "I did it, now I'm saved."

Sadly, I've met many such people who never grew in their new life. Birth is not just an event. Would you celebrate the birth of your baby and then walk off and leave it to itself?

Those who are born from above are just beginning the new life. They have just entered the Kingdom. Be one of those who continue to let Jesus grow within you.

Is this concept shocking? Yes, at least it is the first time you hear it. Nick's jaw was hanging open as Jesus spoke to him. Jesus told him not to be shocked at this idea of being born from above.[73]

---

[73] John 3:7, LITV.

Nick came to this Rabbi maybe hoping to improve in his official role as Pharisee and leader. Instead, the Construction Worker from Galilee tells Nick he must tear down what he has been building and join a new structure entirely. The change will be obvious, as distinct as the air filling a newborn child's lungs.

Jesus gives us a glimpse of that defining moment of Spirit birth: "The wind blows where it wishes, and you hear the sound of it, but cannot tell where it comes from and where it goes."[74] You cannot see wind; it is invisible. Your hearing informs you that the wind has come.

Jesus was having fun with the language again (word play is common throughout the Bible). The same word for "wind" also translates as "Spirit" here.[75] Also, the word "sound" can mean "voice" or "speech."[76] Thus, the *Lit Version* says it this way: "The Spirit breathes where He desires, and you hear His voice; but you do not know from where He comes, and where He goes; so is everyone having been generated from the Spirit."[77]

So which translation is right? Both. The double meaning in this passage reveals how the Lord works with us. There is always a deeper meaning than just what you see on the surface.[78]

Just as we know invisible wind by its sound, so the Spirit comes with a sound/voice/speech from above. "So is everyone who is born of the Spirit."[79] This evidence of the Spirit immersion would happen after Jesus's work was done on earth.[80] There is much, much more to learn here. Since we are following

---

74 John 3:8, NKJV.

75 From the Greek "pneuma."

76 From the Greek "phonē."

77 John 3:8, LITV.

78 You do not have to master Greek or Hebrew to understand it though, you just need to have the Master.

79 John 3:8, NKJV.

80 See Acts 2:1-4, 33, 37-39. We will talk in depth about this later.

the chronology of the Gospels, this book will not rush ahead of Jesus's progressive revelation of His plan.

Nick did not understand and Jesus did not give any more details. However, by the time we conclude the Gospel story, this part will be stunningly obvious. The puzzle pieces snap together at His ascension. Patience, patience. You can't rush revelation.

What is clear here is that humans need a factory reset. Our Creator does not trust us the way we are. To be complete humans in a two-way trust relationship with Jesus, we need the download from above. No amount of earthly improvements will qualify us. Your hardware has to have the new software from above. Those who are children of God use a different operating system.

When a person has been transformed from darkness to light, the difference is obvious. We learn to hear His voice (Spirit) in the inaudible room of our hearts. The Spirit of God leads those born of Him.[81]

Sadly, Pastor Nick didn't get it. He asked, "How are these things able to occur?"[82] Jesus has gone over his head. His spiritual eyes are out of range.

This is part of Jesus's trademark technique: to challenge us to focus on beauty we have never seen before. No one had been born of the Spirit at this point. Jesus was preparing Nicodemus for what was coming.

Imagine getting a job to provide for your family. You are happy to have an income and give them the things they need. Then, you get promoted. The business expands and you have to come up with new ideas, make schedules, and lead transition. Overworked and stressed, picture yourself yelling at your children and telling your spouse to leave you alone so you can

---

[81] Romans 8:14.
[82] John 3:9, LITV.

focus on your work. In such a too-real-to-life scenario, your work became more important than the reason you began it.

We are that ridiculous if we make church about the music, the offering, the youth programs, the building campaign, and other things so much that we forget about God. Has your religion eclipsed Him? Many Christian religions oppose the message of Spirit birth, leaving their followers trying to do God-things in human power.

Nice guy, that Nick, but he couldn't see the Kingdom. Jesus said, "You are the teacher of Israel, and you do not know these things?"[83] The same question still haunts religious experts today who are missing this foundation. Like Nick, I could lead a congregation and still go to hellfire. Religion can become my focus if I am not in the Kingdom.

Jesus said everyone must be born from above. If I am not born of water and Spirit I am not in the Kingdom. I am not from above just because I have begun to believe in Jesus.

---

[83] John 3:10, LITV.

LIKE A SERPENT?

NICODEMUS DID NOT ACCEPT what Jesus said about being born from above. Some people may have already quit reading this book because of that concept. Old Nick, along with others in the same herd of religious professionals, had also rejected John's witness about Jesus.

Speaking for Himself and John, Jesus said, "That which we know, we speak; and that which we have seen, we testify. And you do not receive our testimony."[84] Jesus and John both knew and saw, but this religious man did not accept their eyewitness accounts.

The Gospel of John's literary arrangement ties this conversation to the story of John at the beginning. John the Baptizer came as a witness. John came immersing people in water. Nicodemus had rejected his witness and his water birth.

---

[84] John 3:11, LITV. Here is further evidence that "born of water" referred to John's ministry and "born of Spirit" referred to Jesus's work (John 1:33). Jesus has John in view in all He is saying here because Nick has accepted Jesus's ministry but was one of those who rejected John's (John 1:19, 24).

Many people want Jesus but are not ready for Him to be their King.

When a home builder trusts a foundation, he will build the whole house on that foundation. If, however, a foundation is crumbling or massively off-level, you do not entrust the frame of a house on it. If we find Jesus to be solid and trustworthy, we will build everything into Him—our home, business activities, daydreams, and all else.

Nicodemus was one of those who believed, but not fully. To Jesus, this means a person does not believe at all: "If I tell you earthly things, and you do not believe, how will you believe if I tell you heavenly things?"[85] He said this to the man who saw something great in Jesus, but not clearly.

Nick did not understand the earthly things Jesus spoke about. So far, Jesus had spoken of tearing down the Temple and rebuilding it in three days. He had spoken about being born from above. And most recently, He spoke about hearing the sound of the Spirit.

John had witnessed to water birth and Jesus to Spirit birth. From our perspective, we might think of Spirit birth as heavenly, in another dimension. To the eyes of the One from above, however, these are earthly concepts—easy to grasp.

To humans, immersion in the Spirit might feel like the apex of human experience. In the eternal Kingdom, no one will be born of the Spirit. That only happens while we are here, on earth. If that is just the beginning, then think how huge heavenly things must be!

Those who have been born from above are complete—just as a newborn is a fully complete human. Though wholly human, a newborn is not yet mature. We start with the new birth but must mature into all our potential.

---

[85] John 3:12, LITV.

If we cannot get the simple truths of the Kingdom now, how will we ever handle the "big stuff"? The Lord has so much more He wants to unveil to us. Popular Christianity has ignored or misunderstood Jesus's words, just like the religion pro sitting in front of Him.

Spiritual confusion has spawned the "pray and get saved" ideology. It has redefined terms like "born again." How can modern Christianity ever see the heavenly stuff if it is getting the earthly stuff wrong?

Jesus speaks of being the One from heaven—a place permanently fixed in the Jewish mind as "above." Jesus explains that He is the Son of Man and is in heaven.[86] This changes up the popular Christian myth that heaven is only a place for after death. In the flesh, Jesus lived in the supernatural realm.

You didn't get it before, Nick, so get this: Jesus didn't leave "from above" (heaven). He brought heaven with Him so we could be born from above. We can live above the things of this earth! Are you living "under the circumstances"? What are you doing down there?

When saying "no one has ascended to heaven,"[87] Jesus dismantled a legend about Moses ascending to heaven. Our Lord Jesus had personal experience in heaven—as the Lord God, of course, not in flesh—and was in that realm at that moment. Why did Nick need to hear that? Because Jesus is the only one authorized to talk about heaven.

Their hero Moses only wrote about the Kingdom of Israel. He did not have access to the Kingdom of Heaven when he was writing. Thus, Jesus is on a much higher level than that Pharisee or his hero.

---

[86] See John 3:13.

[87] John 3:13, NKJV.

Moses was quite the deal in his day, but the religion pros were living in the past and missed the Promise before them. They were looking for new apps for their Moses "operating system," not a factory reset with a new OS altogether. Jesus then informed Good Saint Nick that the role of Moses was to prepare the people for the coming of the Son of Man.[88]

Calling Himself "Son of Man," Jesus was playing on words again. The phrase "son of man" would be like someone today saying "human being." Jesus identified with being a common individual among many.

The phrase "Son of Man" also comes from visions by Daniel.[89] In the book of Daniel, the Son of Man came from among humankind, represented humankind, and received "dominion and glory and a kingdom, That all peoples, nations, and languages should serve Him."[90] By using that prophetic term, Jesus identified Himself as the King over all humanity, whose reign would never end.

Most humans have not given their allegiance to King Jesus. Right now, we get to voluntarily give Him dominion in our lives. The following event illustrates how we reset our focus.

While crunching sand underfoot through the wilderness, the people following Moses stopped believing in him. They began to grumble against God and against Moses for dragging them out in the middle of nowhere to die of thirst or hunger. Like their poisoned tongues, poisonous serpents began to bite them and they would die.

When the people cried out and confessed their wrongdoing, Yahweh told Moses to make a bronze serpent. Then, "Moses lifted up the serpent in the wilderness" on a post where

---

[88] See John 3:14.

[89] See Daniel 7:13-14.

[90] Daniel 7:14, NKJV

they could see it.[91] People poisoned by the fiery snakes would have to look up. By seeing the model of what was killing them, they could be healed.[92] The perishing people had no other rescue than to look at what was lifted up.

Using that story as a springboard, Jesus showed that He must be lifted up, too. Sinful humans poison each other. How can a human rescue us from ourselves? Because He is from above.

We look up to the One made in the likeness of sinful flesh, yet in whom is no poison.[93] Those who are "believing into Him should not perish, but have everlasting life."[94] Moses's post only restored earthly life. Jesus's post brings heavenly life.

Already we have a few signals about the cross that is coming. Simeon warned Mary how her heart would be torn by what would happen to Jesus. John first announced that Jesus was the Lamb to be sacrificed for all. Jesus said they would destroy His temple. Now, He shows that He will be lifted up on a pole.

We must see this Man, not keep looking to Moses. If a person does not "see" by being born from above, he or she will not overcome the sting of death, like those poisoned by the serpents. We must see Jesus, the One lifted up higher than any other.[95]

Jesus placed Nick, and every other religious guru, among the unbelievers dying with serpent bites in the wilderness. Satan had stung Nick, and he would have to see Jesus or he would perish, too! The help only comes from above.

---

[91] John 3:14, LITV.

[92] See Numbers 21:4-9.

[93] See Romans 8:3; II Corinthians 5:21; Galatians 3:13.

[94] John 3:15, LITV.

[95] See Isaiah 52:13; Philippians 2:9.

Now we can look at the most-quoted verse in the Bible. Come with me and see how it has been handled by spiritually blind leaders. What Nick just heard will explain it for us.

GOD LOVED LIKE THAT

I F A SNAKE BIT YOUR LEG, you would immediately look at the wound. Fear would keep you focused on the problem. You would have to force yourself out of that stupor to get help.

With Moses, the people had to reset their focus from down to up. One day you decided to stop looking at the poison of sin. You looked up to the One without sin who could rescue you from certain death.

Nicodemus was not looking up. Jesus ended his conversation with him by reminding him about the brass snake on the pole.[96] Confused, Nick slipped out of the Light and back into the darkness he came with.

---

[96] John 3:16, LITV. Some typesetters put this verse in red print or inside quotation marks as if Jesus continued saying these things to Nicodemus (from verse 16 to 21). However, the language shift and the summary statement indicates that this is the narrator (John) speaking again. Jesus did not speak of Himself as having died already. The past tense of "He gave" comes from the voice of John, writing a few decades after the crucifixion. Other examples of John offering a summary to a quote from Jesus come in John 2:21 and 7:39.

The narrator summarizes what just happened: "For God so loved the world that He gave His only begotten Son, that everyone believing into Him should not perish, but have everlasting life." One might think the most quoted scripture in the Bible needs no explanation, but...

The Gospel of John offered this commentary to help us understand what Jesus just said about Moses and the serpent he lifted up. So many people who quote John 3:16 imply that it means, "God loved the world so much that He killed His Son." That is not a correct translation and that statement does not make good logic or theology. Like Nick, many miss the point here.

It is not accurate to understand "God so loved" to mean He loved "so much." In the original text, the word "so" does not mean "so much" but "in such a way" or "in this manner."[97] God loved us, like so.

When you go to an airport, you can look up on the arrival and departure board to find the plane you need. God loved you like that, to put up a destination screen for you to find your way: the only begotten Son. Driving down the highway, you look up and see a big green sign telling you which exit to take to reach your destination. Because God loved you, you can look up to the Son to get out of the dangers and craziness of life.

God loves all the world and wants every human saved from the poison of sin. Moses's pole of healing showed a glimpse of the restoration that would happen to humanity with Jesus on a pole (the cross). Thus, the *New Living Translation* says, "For this is how God loved the world: He gave..."[98]

To be rescued from certain destruction, we must "see" Jesus. They looked to the brass serpent on the pole; we look to

---

[97] The Greek word is "*houto*" and is properly translated "in this manner." Never does it mean "so much."

[98] John 3:16, NLT.

Jesus. This is not like going out and seeing the whales. If you go out whale watching you'll be disappointed if you don't see one come to the surface. If you do not see Jesus—truly come to know Him and understand who He is—you will be devastated.

Just as the bronze serpent became the way for those Hebrews to be saved from death, the Son also rescues a perishing world. All who see Him will live. And to see this King and His Kingdom, we must be born from above!

There's another issue we must address regarding John 3:16. Some have turned the phrase "only begotten Son" into "unique Son." However, the underlying words behind "only begotten" or "only sired" simply mean that a father has generated one child—an only child.[99]

Jesus is the only physically generated Son of God. Adam was son of God by creation, but Jesus by procreation. This makes sense with the story of the Baby born in Bethlehem of a virgin named Mary. For her, however, Jesus was her Firstborn,[100] not her only Son.

What was the mission of the Son? Not to put the world to death as the serpents did, "but that the world might be saved through Him."[101] Jesus has come so we can be rescued, not so we could be destroyed. Those who reject Him are already condemned (doomed), but the "one believing into Him is not condemned."[102]

Jesus does not have to condemn (or poison) humans. Those who reject Him are already poisoned. This includes

---

[99] Using the same word in Luke 7:12, the Scriptures introduce a woman who had lost her only son. He was not unique from other sons but her lone heir. Also in Luke 9:38, a man had an only child. This boy was not distinct from the man's other children but simply his only one.

[100] See Matthew 1:25 and Luke 2:7.

[101] John 3:17, LITV.

[102] John 3:18, LITV.

anyone, like Nick, who is building on their religious foundation instead of Jesus.

Jesus came as light in a dark world. That dark world included the religious community at Jerusalem. Comfortable in their darkness, many complained about the Light getting in their eyes. Nicodemus was still in the dark.

Would jolly old Saint Nick stay in the night, not realizing the true gift from the Father? Or would he step into the Light? Time will tell. We will hear about him again, much later.

So, "the one not believing has already been condemned, for he has not believed into the name of the only begotten Son of God."[103] We use the word "believe" to mean a mushy thing that can change with emotions or from one moment to the next. That is not the kind of belief Jesus seeks.

The Hebrew root for "believe" signifies something of structure or something built solid.[104] Jesus was not encouraging emotional whims of belief like some people had when they saw the signs Jesus did. He was calling Nicodemus to a substantial, foundation change in his own identity.

The things we are discussing in this lesson will cause some to run away. They will want to run back to their familiar "pray and get saved" religion. They will look to their tradition instead of looking up to Jesus. Sadly, they will also face "judgment, that the Light has come into the world, and men loved the darkness more than the Light, for their works were evil."[105]

---

[103] John 3:18, LITV.

[104] The Hebrew verb "*âman*." Note the visual similarity to the Hebrew noun "'*âmên*" from which we get our word "amen," meaning "verified" or simply "yes!" In John 12:38, we find the Greek word "*pisteuo*" used to translate this Hebrew verb "*âman*" from Isaiah 53:1. Interestingly, Jesus introduced this John 3 dialogue with "Amen, amen" which is translated as "Truly, truly" or "I tell you the truth."

[105] John 3:19, LITV.

Like the defenders of God in Jerusalem, many "Christians" will not like the Truth. Loving darkness, they will reject the plain words of Jesus and hide from the light.[106] By preserving their non-committed "belief" in Jesus, they can continue in sin.

Others want to make God in their own image. They have defined religion in a way they find comfortable and then condemn others who do not line up with their preferences. Like those vipers, they poison others with criticism or permissiveness. True religion helps others look up and see Jesus.

Many people today love darkness. They will use science if they feel it backs up their sinfulness. They will dump scientific evidence though if it goes against their cause. We have a world full of darkness that does not want to come to the light lest their evil deeds be exposed.

We also find a world of lawlessness inside religious systems. Manmade religions use Scriptures that support their values but ignore the passages that contradict them. Jesus's main opponents were not the godless, immoral Romans but the people of God who had lost their way.

Too many people are doing religion to try to bring a little glow to the darkness. Jesus offers brilliant light, not just a little less darkness. There is a sharp contrast here just like the difference between the old life and being born from above. It is an abrupt, volatile change.

A person born from above is noticeably different. Their thinking comes from another place than it used to. Their desires and interests have been reset toward that which is from above.

Fortunately, there are those who are done with perishing. Such a person who is "doing the truth comes to the Light, that his works may be revealed, that they exist, having been worked in

---

[106] See John 3:20.

58

God."[107] Though they are not perfect, the Spirit shifts them toward a new identity which they grow into over the following months.

Such individuals know it takes Spirit power to walk in the Light. They are through with their religious tradition and they want something powerful. They want to walk in that fullness of new birth. They want to experience the Spirit breath in their lungs. They want to be born—remade in God's image.

I believe you are one of those.

---

[107] John 3:21, LITV.

BELIEVE INTO JESUS!

T HE GIANT SEQUOIA TREE stretches its green-needle-covered branches over 300 feet into the air. Its roots dig twelve feet deep into the ground and spread as wide as an acre. That relationship between tree and earth teaches us about belief. You are the tree and Jesus is your life source. That's belief.

Here's what believe is not. A girl opens a fortune cookie and hopes the positive vibes she feels mean the random message will come true. A salesman reads his horoscope and crosses his fingers that he will land a big account this month. While neither of those scenes illustrate faith, modern Christianity has accepted the kind of belief that is a flutter in your heart or a wisp of imagination sprinkled with a Bible verse.

Real belief has deep roots. It grabs ahold of substance. Belief does not arise from a figment of one's imagination or by claiming big things and positive-speaking it into existence.

Do you trust the Scriptures like a house trusts itself to a foundation? Do your roots spread an acre wide in Jesus? Or do winds of despair knock over your wispy optimism?

Biblical belief only comes with proof or a promise. Those born from above will see life differently and live in a whole new realm. Too many call themselves Christian today yet all they have is a flimsy feeling to go on. They said the prayer, they walked the aisle, or they shook the preacher's hand. But do they have the substance of Jesus?

After Nicodemus walked out, Jesus continued looking for people He could believe in. He left Jerusalem but worked in the land of Judea (the region surrounding Jerusalem) for a while. There He made disciples and washed them.[108]

The preaching and disciple-making of Jesus and John overlapped each other for a time. John moved north and continued immersing in a place called Aenon on the other side of the Jordan River, a land also called Perea.[109] This dual effort at making disciples lasted for a short time.

Something astounding happened there which has changed my thinking about religion entirely. John the Washer led a huge revolution. The whole countryside went to see John in the months leading up Jesus launching His ministry.[110]

John had trained his disciples and prepared them to look for Jesus. Then, the fighting started. John's group became significant enough that the influencers in Judaism began to argue with them and not just John.

Of course they all meant well. They wanted to be pure before the Lord.[111] Different sects had their own patent on purification: Pharisees had ritual washings of items and such,

---

[108] See John 3:22. As explained in depth in *Seeing Jesus*, the original Greek word for "baptize" means to plunge, immerse, and wash.

[109] See John 3:23.

[110] Most likely, John's public ministry did not last over a year. According to Luke 3:1, John began speaking the word of the Lord in the wilderness in the fifteenth year of Tiberius. If the date of this Roman emperor's ascension is correct at 14 AD, then Jesus's ministry began very soon afterward. John may have only ministered for a few months.

[111] See John 3:25.

Essenes had daily immersions in mikvehs, and John pushed people under the water for the cleansing of their sin. God authorized John's method, but those from different religious tribes wanted to battle with him and his followers about how to be cleansed.

It scares me to see how quickly John's disciples slipped into this mode. They lowered themselves to argue against the establishment rather than continue to help purify those looking for a better life. Your fresh faith and spiritual lift from seeing Jesus will quickly fade into a crusty debate if you don't stay close to Him. John's disciples should have been turning to follow Jesus, not just defend their belief system.

The religious dogmatists came to John and tattled, "Teacher, the One who was with you beyond the Jordan, to whom you have witnessed, behold, this One baptizes, and all are coming to Him."[112] Perhaps this was to tempt John to feel a twinge of jealousy.

He was still calling out and training people to prepare their hearts for the Kingdom. Yet, one part of a person's flesh craves the attention, approval, and power from having followers. Was John struggling to let go? You and I will have to grapple with a temptation to hold our followers to ourselves rather than release them to Jesus.

Not only do people cling to followers out of a craving for validation, but many also invent ministries that have not been inspired by God. That does not give them power. Like the Jerusalem elite, some posers today show off titles and manmade positions but lack true authority.

How did John respond to their temptation for him to confront the ministry of Jesus? He said, "A man is able to receive nothing unless it has been given to him from Heaven."[113] You

---

[112] John 3:26, LITV.
[113] John 3:27, LITV.

can't invent a legitimate religion. John explained to his provokers that Jesus had the goods—He was working in a God-given role.

While writing this, I pause. Why am I writing this? Was this writing assignment born from above? I believe it was. But I will revisit that question often and others like it in everything I do.

We cannot receive an assignment unless it has been given to us from above. You thought you could volunteer for the Kingdom? Wrong. You get assigned to your post; the King decides our role. Amazingly, when you do it, you will love it.

You also must train for your mission. Many have gotten this wrong because they tried to do their mission without His training. It's one thing to wear a shiny police badge but it's better to have gone to the law enforcement academy first. Doing things without assignment or training from Heaven will make your life seem like it is from the other place.

John told them he had joy, not strife because of Jesus. Doing what the King assigns you to do puts a little lift in your spirit. He reminded them that he was not the Anointed One, but his role was to come introduce Him.[114] He had not lost the focus of his role; don't you dare either.

John explained his role with something they understood well: the friend of the bridegroom. Of course, the groom has the joy of marrying the bride. "But the friend of the bridegroom, standing and hearing him, rejoices with joy because of the bridegroom's voice."[115]

The friend of the bridegroom would have been like a best man today, although more involved like a maid/matron of honor often is in American weddings. The best man does not come to a

---

[114] See John 3
[115] John 3:29, LITV.

wedding to compete with the groom but to celebrate with him and make the wedding a success.

The bridegroom's BFF would stand in front of the door to the chamber where the newlywed couple spent their first night. Awkward, for sure. The groom would shout to the best man that the marriage had physically commenced and all was legitimate (meaning she was indeed a virgin and marriageable, TMI, sorry). The groom's friend would then announce this joyous information to the wedding party who could all start celebrating together.

John as much as says, "This is why I'm happy."[116] The wedding was never about the best man. John knew he only played a supporting role in preparing for the Lord's big moment. His words must be our mindset as well while we learn to follow Jesus. Those we lead must see Jesus better and less of us.[117]

Religions do not like to release people to Jesus. Religious groups dogmatically attacked John and then pitted him against Jesus. Religion is a drug.

People struggle to get off drugs because drugs alter reality. The emotional effects of drugs hold many people captive until the Lord sets them free. Religion does, too.

Even manmade religions are effective, though most do nothing to improve your eternity. They make a difference in your emotions. You feel good for attending, obeying, doing.

Many Pharisees saw the difference in their lives because of obeying the clean-up commands. How could they ever leave that? What they did not realize was that they had become loyal to something with some good effects but that was lethal in the long run. What about the Sadducees? Temple worship would not exist without them, right? But the money grab and power-seeking were killing true worship.

---

[116] See John 3:29.
[117] See John 3:30.

People today become loyal to the religious system that told them, "Just pray this prayer and you are saved," or whatever other dogma they follow. Why? An emotional effect can be enough to convince a person they have the right thing.

The mind-altering religious substance traps them, even if it is only 10% pure. They fear leaving what they have known. They cannot believe all those nice people could be wrong. They follow something not given to them from Heaven, and they might have hell in their future.

During the mid-1900's a preacher named William Branham appeared to be a man sent from God, like John. Miracles and healings occurred wherever he went. From outside appearances, his ministry became so powerful he shifted his focus from Jesus and the Kingdom to the wonder of the healings happening at his hands. He claimed to be like Elijah and said he was God's appointed man to say the name of the Lord correctly, which would bring Him back to earth. He presented several false doctrines that his disciples still cling to today.

John had to continue releasing his disciples to Jesus. Parents have to release their children to Jesus. If He calls them to take the message of Jesus overseas, we have to let them go. They become His not ours. As we learn to make disciples, our goal must always be to get them to follow Jesus—He must increase. They must learn to see Jesus and hear from Him for themselves.

In a few of the previous chapters, we looked at Jesus through the eyes of Elder Nick. He represented the religious majority view. Jesus told him, "You people do not accept our testimony."[118] He also said, "I spoke to all of you about earthly

---

[118] Not an exact quote of John 3:11, but Jesus used the plural "you" and was not speaking only to Nicodemus.

things and you do not believe; how then will you believe if I speak of heavenly things?"[119]

The writer of this Gospel brings us back to this thought with a well-mapped message:

> The One having come from above is above all.
> > The one being of the earth is earthy,
> > and speaks of the earth.
> The One coming out of Heaven is above all.[120]

Are you putting your roots into the things of earth? Sink your roots into the words of Jesus, the identity of Jesus, the life of Jesus. Imagine how much higher the Redwood would grow if its roots were planted above. Trees cannot grow in the sky, though, because they are of the earth. Same with you and me.

This is the reset. It takes a heavenly seed to grow in heavenly "soil." You cannot just take an earthly thing and stick it in the sky. Neither can you take a human and stick him or her in heaven.

We must be born from above:

- Darkness to light,
- Wrath to peace,
- Sadness to joy,
- Death to life.

Jesus, the one "from above" or "on top," is over all. John, by contrast, is earthly—Nick did not receive the earthly things and so missed the heavenly. John confirms that which is "from above" is from heaven—the terms are synonymous.

How is Jesus from above? Not just because of a miraculous conception from above, but because He is God-made-

---

[119] Again, words changed to show the plural focus of His words in John 3:12.
[120] John 3:31, LITV.

flesh. John knew Jesus's true identity as the Yahweh for whom he was preparing the way. Jesus, as both God and Son of Man, is from heaven and in heaven.

Although He spoke of the things He had personal knowledge of, "no one" (generally speaking) received His testimony.[121] Jesus came to share truths from above. He invites us to join Him there by becoming what He is.

The person who receives His message "has sealed that God is true."[122] Have you certified God as true? It is not enough that He is true; as humans, we must verify Him as true. To accept the message and person of Jesus is to sign onto God's plan.

---

[121] See John 3:32.
[122] John 3:33, LITV.

GOODBYE, COMFORT ZONE

A PROPHET USED TO BRING a message to people in a particular place: Jerusalem, for example. Where does Jesus's message extend to? If we had any question about that, the Scripture explains that the "One whom God sent speaks the Words of God, for God does not give the Spirit by measure."[123]

A prophet, such as John the Washer, had a designated realm of influence: a city or a country, particularly. Jesus, however, had no limits. He came to take away the sin of the world.[124] His region has no limit and no other prophet could do His work: remove sin, give new life. With Jesus, we got more than a message.

The Jews worried that Jesus overstepped His boundaries. Not only does John explain that He has no border restraining Him, but shows that rather than being opposed to the plan of God, Jesus fulfills it perfectly: "The Father loves the Son and has given all things into His hand."[125]

---

[123] John 3:34, LITV.
[124] See John 1:29.
[125] John 3:35, LITV.

The religious figure heads must have exploded at this idea of a human having the final say in everything. Not only does Jesus have the "upper hand" in this world, He is from the upper level. The Son is the very manifestation of the life of the Father in human form.[126]

You are more than a tree, but to visit that idea once more, if you believe (get planted) into the highly favored Son, you live forever![127] You have seen enough death in your lifetime to know that physical life is fragile. By being born from above, you become planted into a Life that never ends. This is not something you can obtain physically.

Religions often present all kinds of qualifiers for self-improvement. Most of them are good changes to make, but if we get the idea that we can improve our behavior until we are eternal, we are most sadly lost. The person who continues "disobeying the Son will not see life, but the wrath of God remains on him."[128]

Many English versions do a disservice to John 3:36 by contrasting the two phrases: "one who believes" and the "one who does not believe." In the original, however, these are not both the same words for "believe" with one simply having a "not" added on. The negative term for "not believe"[129] can be also translated as 'to disobey, to not be persuaded, to refuse belief and obedience.'

Those who do not believe are in willful disobedience. Those who believe will obey Jesus and His commands. A disciple desired to have the rabbi's dust on himself. Walking close behind the rabbi, they could learn how he spoke and imitate him. We, who are born-from-above, sync our lives with Jesus!

---

[126] See John 1:4; I John 1:1-3; 5:11, 20; Colossians 1:19; 2:9; Hebrews 1:3.
[127] See John 3:36.
[128] John 3:36, LITV.
[129] Greek *apeitheo*.

Evidence of this new life is in the doing. Those who do not obey cannot see, are not born into the Kingdom, and face the day of God's rage. Those born from above belong to Heaven and live at peace with God. Notice the chilling parameters of either sinking ourselves into Jesus or disobeying him. We must be born and live from above.

Today, there is strong move to silence the voice of believers in Jesus from speaking out to social or political causes in our world. A few years ago, Nathaniel Haney spoke against the spirit and practices of Islam. Many criticized him for saying, "If you've never been out of this country and you've never been to a Muslim country, you don't understand how dark Islam is. People don't understand how bad Islam is."[130]

One person in the audience that day videoed part of his sermon and posted it to social media. She claimed to be afraid for Muslim people who might be victims of acts of hate because of these words. However, another media outlet picked up the story and likened Pastor Haney to early explorers whom public sentiment would not believe because they were going against popular beliefs. The piece states, "let us remember what Saudi Arabia does to women who drive a car (beatings or death), men who disobey sharia law (beatings or death), homosexuals (beating or death), and so on down the line. . . . For most of us, beatings and death is pretty dark stuff."[131]

While we should be kind with our words and understanding toward our listeners, believers in truth should not

[130] Shirin Rajaee, "Stockton Pastor Accused Of Delivering Hateful Sermon About Islam," CBS Sacramento, Feb 2, 2017, https://sacramento.cbslocal.com/2017/02/02/stockton-pastor-accused-of-delivering-hateful-sermon-about-islam/

[131] Sam Di Gangi, "Christian Pastor Now Under Attack After A Sermon He Gave Left Some In His Town Feeling Outraged," Conservative Daily Post, Feb 9, 2017, https://conservativedailypost.com/christian-pastor-now-under-attack-after-a-sermon-he-gave-left-some-in-his-town-feeling-outraged/

avoid speaking clearly into a world adrift in moral and spiritual confusion. Should a person speak out on social or religious issues? Look now at how, where, and why we should be bold for our faith.

John the Immerser chose to give some straight talk to the leader of the land. Herod Antipater (called more often "Antipas") was married to Phasaelis, the daughter of the ruler of the Nabatean kingdom, on Israel's southwest border. He insulted her, her father Aretas, and their kingdom by divorcing her and taking Herodias as his wife. Already disputing about borders with the Galilean ruler, King Aretas fought against Herod Antipas and defeated his army.

John did not stay silent about this politician's moral issues. The defeat by King Aretas was not enough of a blow to Antipater's ego. John told him, "It is not lawful for you to have your brother's wife"[132] (who also was his niece). Moses had instructed the people that a man should never marry a woman who had been married to his brother.[133]

John was jailed for speaking what the Lord told him to speak, regardless of whether it was politically correct. This put him in the class of other heroic prisoner-prophets such as Jeremiah and Micaiah from centuries before.[134] Herod Antipas wanted to kill John for what he said, but did not want bad press—the common folk saw John as a prophet.[135] Lady Herodias wanted to kill him, too, but did not have a legitimate reason for execution.[136]

Herod and Herodias did not like the idea of a factory reset. They knew that to live in harmony with God would require

---

[132] Mark 6:18, NKJV.

[133] See Leviticus 18:16; 20:21.

[134] See I Kings 22:7-14; Jeremiah 20:2; 37:15.

[135] See Matthew 14:5.

[136] See Mark 6:19.

massive changes in their lives—separation from one another, to begin with. This is why many people do not take the factory reset option today: they do not want to change their ways. They didn't want to feel the pain of giving up what they love.

However, Herod appreciated someone who would preach it straight. People are hungry to hear the truth undiluted. There are lot of feel-good preachers who say not to change anything. People do not value a wimpy message, even if it makes them feel good.

Herod noticed John's pure and powerful life and did not want anything to happen to him. Herod loved to hear John speak.[137] Like many today, he loved the preaching but never lived it. The belief in Herod's heart was not rooted, just whimsical.

John left his comfort zone to do what mattered in the long run. His desire to decrease had come to pass in an awkward way. Someone said that serving God is the best life possible. It might also be the shortest life possible. Would John have called out Clinton? Obama? Trump?

When leaders live in sin, it trickles down. A leader needs to be a moral leader. John does not excuse the man just because he is not in a biblical role, but pointed out several other evils Herod had done.[138]

John wouldn't have said, "Well, a President isn't a pastor. A Senator isn't a saint." These governmental leaders are God's ministers.[139] Wife swapping is wrong.

---

[137] See Mark 6:20. Some versions have this verse to say Herod "kept him safe" and "did many things" in response to his preaching. However, scholars argue those same words could be read that Herod "observed him" and "was much perplexed." The story bears out the internal struggle John had between wanting to be like John and not wanting to leave his godless marriage.

[138] See Luke 3:19.

[139] See Romans 13:4.

MAKE THE MOMENT

WHEN HEROD CAPTURED JOHN, a new phase of ministry began. Jesus traveled back into the region of Herod Antipas, where John had recently been working.[140] Down in the Jordan River, the muddy water swirled around those committing to follow Jesus. Meanwhile, the religious snobs started making an issue of how Jesus had baptized more people than John had.[141]

Can you imagine being baptized by Jesus Himself? You couldn't have. "Jesus Himself did not baptize," but His disciples did it in His place.[142] When a disciple was commissioned to do a work for the rabbi, it was as if the rabbi himself were doing the work. Thus, when Jesus's disciples immersed new believers, they were washed by Jesus.

The same is true today: Jesus's appointed representatives can immerse others into Jesus as His disciples. John's baptism is

---

140 See Matthew 4:12.
141 See John 4:1.
142 See John 4:2. In Acts 19:2-6, we see Jesus's "washing" replaces John's.

now obsolete,[143] but we can receive the washing away of sins that comes by that Name above every other name.[144] Jesus didn't just come to wash with the Spirit, but He continued and fulfilled the water immersion John began.

Coming back into Galilee to announce the good news of God's Kingdom,[145] Jesus stayed on the alert for mob mentality. An extreme of either too many people against Him could cause His death to come too quickly. Also, too many people cheering for Him would also bring an early death at the hand of the jealous religious leaders.

Working His way north, He had to stop in Samaria first. A need drew Him there. If He had wanted to avoid the place, He could have gone the long way around.

The Samaritans descended from the Jews who had married among the Assyrians. Gentiles thought of them as Jews, but the Jews thought of them as non-Jews. Thus, they became their own isolated group. Racism notwithstanding, they needed Jesus.

Samaria marched to a different religious drumbeat. They did follow the writings of Moses but observed Hebrew holidays on different days than the Jews. If travelers were to stop in Samaria to eat, they might find that no one would sell to them if the Samaritans were celebrating a holy day of their own.

Do you find certain people groups unusual or even disgusting, like the disciples did the Samaritans? Those folks needed someone to love them enough to share the truth. Their religion did no more for the Samaritans than the traditions of the Pharisees and Sadducees did for the Jews.

---

[143] See Acts 19:2-6.

[144] See Acts 2:38; 22:16; I Peter 3:21.

[145] See John 4:3 with Mark 1:14.

Why did Jesus come? Why did John go out and share the good news? Because people needed it. What is drawing you from the point of just being a follower of Jesus to being someone who reaches out to others and shows them Jesus? The people around you need Him—that's all the motivation we need!

There are so many other things we could do with our lives, but people need Jesus, even the unlikeable ones. For this reason, Jesus stopped in an unlikely and unlikeable place. Sychar had an interesting past.

Abraham's grandson Jacob purchased a piece of land in the area later called Shechem.[146] There, he had to dig a well to water his flocks.[147] Little did he realize that the Promised One would use that fountain as an object lesson.

Later, a local boy from Shechem raped Jacob's daughter Dinah. So, Jacob's sons tricked the men of the town and killed them in retaliation.

Much later, Jacob's will transferred that piece of ground to Joseph, his favored son who had endured many years of slavery and separation from his family in Egypt.[148] Joseph rescued his relatives from death, like Jesus would do many centuries later. When the people of Israel (Jacob's other name) left Egypt and moved into the Promised Land, they brought their ancestor Joseph's remains to Shechem to bury him.[149]

Traveling northward, Jesus paused for a break in Sychar, a short distance from where the ancient Shechem had once stood. Walking for most of that day had drained Him. Remember, He was probably still rebuilding His strength after not eating for those 40 days.

---

[146] See Genesis 33:19.
[147] See John 4:6.
[148] See John 4:5 and Genesis 48:22-23.
[149] See Joshua 24:32.

He sat on the edge of "Jacob's fountain."[150] The low-walled well plunged over a hundred feet below ground level with a hole dug seven-feet-wide inside.[151] Having an attachment to such ancient history certainly left the locals feeling a sense of belonging in God's story. Their "hero connections" certainly made them feel like they were better than others.

Notice how the setting of this event stands out much differently from the backdrop when Nicodemus visited Jesus. He came at night, when everything was hard to see. He lived in the proud center of everything Jewish. Now, Jesus took a seat in the place Israel's children murdered men in cold blood. He sat down in the middle of the day, when it is easiest to see everything clearly.

A surprise came up the lane: a woman. In every way, she was the opposite of Nicodemus.

We know his name.

We do not know hers.

He was a leader of the Jews.

She was an underdog even to her people.

He was a high-ranking religious official.

She does not appear religious at all.

He was concerned with lofty thoughts of religion.

She was just trying to survive another day.

He came to Jesus when no one would see.

Her life was out in the open.

---

[150] John 4:6, LITV.

[151] Kruse.

Jesus asked for a drink.[152] This was more shocking than we can picture. Jewish men did not speak to Jewish women. Jews hated to deal with Samaritans. So, a Jewish man would certainly not ask a favor of a Samaritan woman.

Awkward!

Jesus was sitting there alone because His disciples had traveled into town to get some sandwiches and munchies.[153] She sensed the oddity of this situation. Clutching her water pot to her chest, she couldn't help but ask Him how on earth He could speak to her.[154]

She identified herself with the label someone else had chosen: "Samaritan woman." She should have known herself as someone more colorful and meaningful, but had resigned herself to accept the label. He didn't seem to notice her social tag.

Do you live under a "Samaritan" label? Do you let things beyond your control define you? Poverty, birthplace, race, gender, and many more things we had no control over can trigger oppressive people to label us.

Our own choices can become a label others tag us with for life. Words like "druggie," "failure," or "rip-off," keep past bad choices stuck to a person. By categorizing us, others can look down on us or try to punish us in some way.

What about how you look at others? Do you label them by their past? She sensed that this Man saw her as a person and did not look down on her like most people did.

---

[152] See John 4:7.
[153] See John 4:8.
[154] See John 4:9.

Are you stereotypical? "Jews do not deal with Samaritans."[155] Yet Jesus stood out from the stereotype of His people. There are similar Christian stereotypes today.

A man looked at a friend of mine one day and said, "Why are you so nice to me? Your people hate me." He knew she was a follower of Jesus.

He continued his tirade: "When they would hire me to run sound for their events, they were all polite on the phone. When they met me in person, they became cold. And every time, one of their people would get up on stage and talk against homosexuality. They never thanked me for how I went out of my way to make everything flawless for their events. They never noticed that I did way more than expected. They just hated me."

My friend was shocked and taken back. She had to apologize on behalf of those people who had hurt their witness for Jesus. Yet his surprise at her kindness was rewarding. He could tell she was different. He saw the love of Jesus in her.

Do you fit the stereotype? Or do you stand out? With one simple sentence, Jesus put Himself in a different league than other Jews. He talked to this woman as a real person. Today, a stereotypical man would talk down to her, objectify her, flirt with her. A male follower of Jesus should stand out from the stereotype.

Many Christians today seek to "fit in" with the culture around them. They want to blend in. You do not win people by imitating them. They must see you as different in a positive way.

Notice another stereotype breaker with Nicodemus and this woman. You would think that a person with enough spiritual hunger to come talk to Jesus would quickly receive His message. Perhaps approaching a person who is just going about their business is not the best way to reach someone. Yet we see the

---

[155] John 4:9, LITV.

opposite of both of these expected outcomes. The seeker went away confused. The unsuspecting person, the Samaritan woman, took the conversation to heart.

Jews and Samaritans would not drink from the same water fountain, so to speak. Who do you not have things in common with? How might the Lord help you bridge the divide between you and them? Could Jesus lead you to overcome a stereotype?

Jesus's conversations appear to be unforgettable. He did not say to the woman, "Is the weather hot enough for ya?" He was not clichéd and predictable.

A follower of Jesus should not be predictable. We will not make a difference in the world if we are like watered-down vanilla. Jesus's words open eyes.

Don't be guilty of dull conversations about meaningless small talk. Jesus took a routine situation and made it unforgettable. How many predictable situations have you been in that could have been life-changing? Learn from Jesus to make every moment count.

You make a good conversation by allowing just enough tension. A person should remember they met you. The conversation should be memorable. Spiritual conversations should feel like a drink of cold water.

KNOW THE GIFT

REMEMBER THAT TIME you bought your family member that expensive, fragile item? Of course, he didn't know what was in that beautifully wrapped box with all those ribbons and the gold-edge "to and from" tag. He kept talking to someone else, waving your box around and setting it down clumsily. You held your breath, wanting to warn him but not wanting to ruin the surprise.

I think Jesus might have felt something like that while watching this woman standing near Him at the well. He even said something like, "If you only knew what the gift of God was..." She was not handling the Gift well. Fortunately, It is not fragile; she was.

She was defensive because she'd had guys use their lines on her before. That's why she was like, "Why are you talking to me?" Would this Man proposition her?

She didn't need another guy asking for her number. She'd been promised the stars a few times now. She just wanted to get water and didn't know why this "guy" was so unaware of the social wall between her race and His.

Why do people wrap up gifts? To hide them. To make that box special and more than just another item on the shelf. To make it personal.

I'm not sure why we hide our gifts, but at birthdays and holidays, it's a thing. Would Jesus wrap things up in such a way we don't see them? Would He hide valuable truths so we could dig in and enjoy them later? Yes.

Do you ever feel like some things in the Bible are hard to understand? You may have just found a gift. Don't throw it out because you don't know what is inside. When the Lord lets you open up that truth, it will be more memorable and meaningful than if you had just found it in plain view.

If you look through the wrapping, you will see that Jesus has the Gift for her. And you. And me. But you cannot see it at first. If He just shoved it in your face, you would not appreciate it as much. It has to be hidden first.

He told her, ""If you knew the gift of God, and who is the One saying to you, 'Give Me to drink,' you would have asked Him, and He would give you living water."[156] Jesus put her at ease by speaking about what she will receive. He really was not there for her to give (the drink of water) but for her to receive.

The Lord got to the point: God's gift. This word gift[157] is the same word in the New Testament used when speaking of the Spirit filling people. In a new way, Jesus was speaking about being born of the Spirit.

You and I read that account and realize how silly it was for her to be worried about pulling another bucketful from the hole

---

[156] John 4:10, LITV, single quotes added for clarity.

[157] The Greek is "*dōrea*" just as used in Acts 2:38; 8:20; 10:45; 11:17. This is different than what have been called the "spiritual gifts" in I Corinthians 12 and 14.

81

in the ground. The Source of Life sat before her, though looking exhausted and weary.

Look at your own life. What are you frazzled about? What are you grabbing at while missing the One who gives the best Gift?

Jesus offered her living water—another hidden reference to the Spirit.[158] It might have been easy for her to overlook this statement because in that culture, they described moving water in rivers, streams, and springs as "living water." For religious purposes, they used "living" water for immersion, washing dishes, and such like.

We should pause here to reflect on the good old days. The days without plumbing in the house. Instead of running water, you had to run for water. I imagine that water being clean, clear, and refreshing.

In that time, cities would spring up around a source of water. Though we need water to survive, I don't think about water much. Except for natural disasters, we do not worry about going without water, but it was a realized need then and any lack of water created an immediate crisis.

Jesus appears to talk like He could come up with water on His own—no well needed. That seems impossible to her. The woman did not understand. Not knowing who He was, she sized Him up, saw He had no vessel to carry water, and concluded, "This guy doesn't know what he is talking about."

She couldn't let it go, though. "Where then do You get that living water?"[159] His arms were not long enough to reach the spring down below. That arid region had no streams nearby.

---

[158] See how Jesus later used this analogy of receiving the Spirit in John 7:37-39. Also, the Old Testament prophets described the Spirit of God as the source of living water in Isaiah 44:3; Jeremiah 2:13; 17:13.

[159] John 4:11, NKJV.

Where does Living Water come from? Above, of course, but she could not see that yet.

She set out to show Him the importance of what is going on, telling Him about her great-great-great-great-great-grandpappy.[160] Who could provide greater water than Jacob who dug this well? It had flowed for about 1,800 years. Who did Jesus think He was to beat a precedent like that?

Jacob could not give them living water, just moving water. Many people mistake movement for something spiritual. That's why so many will not let go of their religion to turn to Jesus. Like the woman at the well, they are steeped in years of religious history. They do not look for Jesus because their past is so impressive.

That well may have been moving and fresh, but it was not alive like what Jesus would provide. This woman was not looking for anything. She needed something more, but she did not think there was anything outside her realm of experience. Old Nick came looking but didn't see. She wasn't even looking.

Her rhetorical question assumed a "no" answer. "You think you are something, buddy? No one could be greater than Jacob." If nothing else, she had learned how to put a forward man in his place.

Jesus set himself up for something impossible. Was He greater than Jacob? Yes. Both Jews and Samaritans would have to see that. Jacob quenched the thirst of his children and livestock; Jesus would bring water to the lost sheep of Israel and then the world.

Does this woman think she is special because of her ancestry? Jesus puts Jacob in the same lot as everyone else: thirsty. Just because he dug a deep well did not mean he found life-giving water.

---

[160] See John 4:12.

Rather than focus on ol' grampy Jake, Jesus turned her attention back to the difference between what Jacob did and what He does. Anyone who drinks of the water from beneath will thirst again. Whoever drinks the water Jesus gives, "will not thirst, never! But the water which I will give to him will become a fountain of water in him, springing up into everlasting life."[161]

This "springing up" also could be translated as "leaping up." Other scriptures use this word[162] to describe paralyzed people who leaped to their feet when healed. When the life-giving water enters you, you'll "leap up" into a new life. Like the sound of the wind, the change will be noticeable.

Jesus did not offer her a sip. This is not just a splash. You don't have to work for this Water, like they had to for the water beneath them at that moment. Jacob could only uncover water that was already moving beneath earth's surface. Jesus brings water that causes us to spring up into a life that is out of this world.

Geysers are water bursts that leap up from underground. As Old Faithful becomes less and less faithful,[163] the people of earth must reach for the sustained fountain. The tense of the verb "leaping up" shows that it does not burst forth from time to time but is an ongoing flow! It continues spurting up into eternity.

Many people today claim to have the "gift" and the "living water" Jesus spoke of but they do not have continuity. Their religion gives them restarts and battery boosts, but not a factory reset. If they had the real thing, it would continually burst forth within them.

---

[161] John 4:14, LITV.

[162] Greek *hallomai*. See Acts 3:8 and 14:10.

[163] The Old Faithful geyser, located in Yellowstone, has developed an irregular schedule over the years.

Many who claim to have new life have other things still leaping up in their lives. Anger springs up. Lust leaps up. Greed bursts forth. Depression builds a steady stream of pressure. Those forces cannot flow with the life-giving water at the same time. Just as one cannot speak blessing and cursing at the same time, so one cannot have evil fruit springing up and good fruit, too.[164]

The conversation changed. "Sir, give me some water."[165] Jesus began by asking her for spring water, now she was begging for springing water. There is no way this woman fully understood what Jesus was saying. She wanted whatever He had, but was still thinking of not having to drag herself out there in the heat.

Perhaps you do not fully understand what it means to have a continual flow springing up in your life, but you want it. I know what it is like to have a geyser experience and think "this changes everything." A few weeks later it hasn't.

Perhaps you have a religious tradition of prayer, devotions, regular church attendance, and such like. Perhaps you have a geyser-type of religious experience where church meetings suddenly cause the Spirit to leap up within you. Imagine moving into the life Jesus describes instead of just trying to sip another spiritual sensation.

The Kingdom is constantly full of this life. Imagine awakening to each day with a steady stream of power from above. Picture a life where love is leaping up within you all day long, where joy bursts from you onto others, a fountain of peace that does not come and go with circumstances, and overflowing patience, kindness, faithfulness, self-control, and much more. Think about living in such a Kingdom awareness where these strengths continually flow through you until the day you enter eternity!

---

[164] See James 3:12 and Galatians 5:19-23.

[165] See John 4:15.

Do you want that? Do you see how dry your life is? Do you see how those dehydrating forces of sin leap up within you to cause you to live in stress, unforgiveness, or insecurity?

Like that Samaritan woman, you must admit you do not have the continual life-giving source. You want this drink that will cause you to never thirst again. Admit that you are tired of spectator religion where you only respond to the Spirit when He is flowing through others. Tell Jesus, "Give me this water so I never thirst again!"

WHAT IS ALIVE IN YOU?

DEEP INSIDE THE HUMAN BRAIN sits a powerful structure driving actions and reactions. Before a child develops cognitive skills and can process information through his or her prefrontal cortex, a system in the midbrain has been running the show for years. Thus, a person can be set with a certain pattern of behavior for life unless something major happens to shift that thinking.

I'm not sure we can even use the word "thinking" when we speak of this limbic system inside our skulls. An almond-shaped organ you will never see has been in action long before you could discern right and wrong. Called the "amygdala," this little organ ties into your emotions and began triggering responses long before other parts of your brain developed. With it, the hippocampus and other parts of the limbic cortex spurred your actions and reactions before you developed the ability to speak or process logic.

In other words, you struggle to put words to your core drives and feelings. Deep inside, literally, these cranial elements drive you to act and react in ways you may have never stopped to reflect on why you do so. Early traumatic situations imprinted you to respond in rage, withdraw in fear, or be driven by guilt.

Why would we discuss neurobiology in a book about knowing Jesus better? I promise you that I do not bring this up because I am an expert in the study of the brain. I defer to my friend Neil Jepson, Ph.D. who has a lot more knowledge and experience in these things. I'm thankful that he's introduced me to many of these concepts so that I could have handles for conversations about things like this that are tough to see and discuss.

Jesus knows you to the core. He sees your triggers, drives, and the function of this central part of your life: the limbic system. The fears, shame, guilt, or anger activated by that part of your body can come under His power.

Why didn't Jesus talk about this organ or teach people about neurobiology? For one, no one would have understood what He was talking about if He had. It was easier to address the popular expression of emotion by referencing the "heart," where many emotions are felt.

Rather than talk about the technicalities of the central nervous system, Jesus targeted it with stories and messages that moved a person, rather than just informed them. Not only did He trigger emotions, but He spoke deep into the spirit of a person in a way that could heal and change even their instinctive responses.

Religious institutions try to get into the conscious brain: information, requirements, and behaviors. Most religions do nothing to heal the inner person. Jesus worked from the inside out. He still does.

Jesus reaches to the core and resets our reflex responses. The details will come later. Once a person has been reset at this very foundation, they will then change their conduct and other essentials of life, too.

Do you "try" to be like Jesus? Does godliness flow from you, or like most religious people, is it something you have to "work at"? The Creator knows how we were made and He knows each of us need to get back to the original factory settings He intended for us. Watch how He did this with the woman at the well.

Jesus said to her, "Go, call your husband, and come here."[166] He knew she didn't have one.

She gulped. I can hear her thinking, "Well, this escalated quickly, but here we are."

Let's pause and look at how Jesus got her to this moment. The conversation began with what she wanted: water. It was a common enough topic, but Jesus had a plan to turn this into a spiritual conversation before He began.

You and I both want to tell people about Jesus. We can learn from Him here. He did not just small talk. Every conversation counts.

Yet, Jesus was not warped and weird when talking to people about their heart need. He did not walk up to random strangers and ask them if they knew Him as their personal Savior. He did not accost pedestrians with, "If you died today, where would you go—heaven or hell?"

Many spiritual conversations feel strange because we focus first on talking to people about what they need: Jesus, salvation, etc. Our Lord began by speaking about what she wanted, and then used that springboard to get to what she needed.

You might know a person, for example, who needs Jesus. Right now, however, this person is not looking for a Bible study, but simply a way to forget the past and be able to sleep at night. They need His Gift as this woman did, but all they know is they want something to make them happy and not hopeless any more.

---

[166] John 4:16, NKJV.

Jesus could take a common thing and turn it into a fascinating, unforgettable conversation. Too often, believers take a fascinating thing and turn it into a boring or awkward thing: "You need to be saved," "God loves you," and so on. When Jesus nudges you to talk with a person, see what they relate to easily.

Some readers get stuck on some of these examples of Jesus's conversations and think that topic is how to approach a person. "You need to be born again" or "You need living water." It means nothing to tell a person they will not have to draw water from a well—they drink from a water bottle. Sometimes people try to describe the Kingdom by talking about sheep, vineyards, and other illustrations Jesus used. However, Jesus used those because people related to them and could understand the application.

The person you are talking with would "get it" better if you talked about the turbo on an engine, remodeling a home, or moving to a new city. Why educate people on distant concepts from the first century when they have illustrations all around them. If we are going to give an unforgettable message about Jesus, we have to speak in a way people comprehend. If Jesus met with that woman today, He might use a thirst-quenching sports drink as an illustration of the Spirit.

I'm sure there was a decided pause before the woman confessed, "I have no husband."[167] Jesus commended her honesty. Like He did with Nathanael and Simon Peter, Jesus knew something about her an ordinary person could not.

Jesus explained to her, "You have had five husbands, and now he whom you have is not your husband. You have spoken this truly."[168] This is the Spirit of prophecy at work. He can give you insight like this too, if He knew you would use it well.

_____

167 John 4:17, NKJV.
168 John 4:18, LITV.

At her wedding, a bride wanted the minister to read I John 4:18. "There is no fear in love; but perfect love casts out fear." The minister accidentally went to John 4:18. "You have had five husbands, and the one whom you now have is not your husband..." The crowd gasped and the bride was horrified. [Insert laughing track.]

Notice how quickly Jesus transitioned that conversation. He spoke in a way she understood about something she wanted. He used that to illustrate her heart need. Next, He spoke to her deepest hurt.

We don't know what happened with those five guys. Did they die? Did they ditch her? Did she leave them? Did they start a burger joint? And who was the dude she was shacking up with anyhow?

Those details don't stop the offer of living water. Jesus is not afraid to reach your hurt and change it. He sees your hidden story. He's not digging for the details. He's not interested in making you miserable but in making you mobile again.

This woman was trapped by her past. Ordinarily, people did not travel to the well in the heat of the day. They went in the cool of the morning. Was she avoiding other people because she couldn't handle her unhealed hurts and those who might poke at them?

She stammered something to sound coherent as the healing balm closed wounds inside. "Sir, I perceive that You are a prophet."[169] Already, she could see more. The reset had begun.

At first she only saw a man who should hate her race. Then she saw a man with an endless water supply. Now she saw a prophet. Keep rubbing your eyes, girl.

---

[169] John 4:19, LITV.

She came for water. Next, she begged Him to let her know more about spiritual things. How did He go from the common to the crucial thing so quickly?

According to author Eugene Schwartz, there are five levels of awareness a person must go through when making a new purchase or adopting a new way of life:

1. Unaware. (They don't know they have a problem)

2. Problem aware. (They don't know there is a solution)

3. Solution aware. (They know they have options)

4. Best solution aware. (They know which one is better)

5. Aware and motivated. (They are ready to change now)

I'm not sure how scientific his ideas are, but that concept helps me map out the progress of an interaction. Perhaps you can think of how this applies to people you are telling about Jesus now.

When we first meet the woman, she did not know she had a problem. Her main concern was quenching her physical thirst. She had not consciously acknowledged that she was spiritually dehydrated and dying.

On the second level, she became aware of her problem (wrecked relationships) but did not know a solution. She most likely lay awake at night and wondered if there was something more to life. She might have been crying herself to sleep. Talking about her husbands, she became more "problem aware."

Third, a person becomes aware that there is a solution. Many people around you are clueless that they have a problem. They just shrug and say, "That's life." Others are aware they have a problem but do not know there is a solution. You see this woman transition to being solution-aware.

Fourth, one must not only be aware of the solutions but also know which one is correct. She started sorting through that next. She had to weigh her religious tradition against what Jesus said.

Finally, a person not only embraces the right solution but also becomes highly motivated to take action. You will see this woman hit level five shortly. Reflect on your recent conversations with those who need Jesus and think about where they are in that journey.

Jesus had now addressed what had been dehydrating that woman. Men had drained her, brought her up empty. Where does she need living water? In her home life, to heal her love life.

She was hiding the problem, but Jesus brought it out into full view: her "husbands," plural. We don't know how many of those ended with a funeral and how many in divorce court. A funeral can break your heart, but a divorce reaches a different level of hurt, taking a piece of it. Jesus does heart surgery.

If we are looking at this story as an example of how to bring someone to Jesus, we just got outclassed. How on earth are we supposed to know things about a person's personal life? We aren't.

There is an important thing we disciples learn from the Rabbi here. We cannot do this. It is not humanly possible to do the work of the Kingdom.

We can pick up tips about speaking to things the person understands. We can help move them from their want to their need. We can help them discover their own problem and the solution in Jesus.

Yet this is a supernatural work. The Kingdom is above. The power comes from above.

His techniques are out of this world. What Jesus does here is use information humanly impossible to know. He had never met this woman before, yet He knows her love life.

You cannot bring people into the Kingdom by a program. The reason we are taking our time through this series is that we are learning a process of how God works, not a bag of tricks to use in all situations.

Can a disciple reach a person on the level Jesus did in Samaria? Of course. He gives us His Spirit to open our understanding. At times, He will give us "inside information" so we can see what is keeping a person from the Lord and what they need Him to do for them.

You might think it would be awkward or uncomfortable to talk to someone about their hurt. If talking to a person about her pain were a bad idea, what would an EMT do? Does the paramedic's manager say, "Don't talk about their broken leg, they will be embarrassed"? If people understand that you can help them, they do not mind opening up and letting you help remove the splinter or set a splint. They must want to be healed.

Jesus addresses the "broken leg" in a healing way. Do you think she wanted to destroy any of those marriages? Not when they started. Regardless of her past, she was worth restoring. So are you. So are the people you meet at the well.

RELIGIOUS OR SPIRITUAL?

THE WOMAN PERCEIVED that Jesus was a prophet. So, she did what a lot of people will do to you when you start talking to them about Jesus: switch on religious talk. Such a person will say, "My grandpa was a preacher" or "Do you believe God flooded the entire earth?" The woman at the well pointed to the ruins of the temple in Mt. Gerizim, saying, "Our fathers worshiped on this mountain, and you Jews say that in Jerusalem is the place where one ought to worship."[170]

When the Hebrew people first entered the Promised Land, they camped at Gerizim and read the writings of Moses.[171] The Samaritans saw themselves as the conservatives who remained true to the original message while the Jews had taken a later location on Mt. Zion, the Temple Mount in Jerusalem. The Jews recognized many more Holy Writings than the Samaritans did. Samaritans were supposedly Moses-only purists, while the Jews read the Psalms, the historical books, and the prophets, too.

---

[170] John 4:20, NKJV.
[171] See Deuteronomy 12:5-11; 27:12.

You have probably started into a spiritual conversation with someone and they jumped to denominational differences. Or they say something like, "Oh, you're a church person, what do you think about blood moons?" This is often a defensive mechanism.

By discussing a larger debate or an existential theory, they put the focus somewhere other than themselves. She did not want to talk about her five husbands or her new feller. She wanted to talk about her preacher grandpa (so to speak) and how her religion is better than Jesus's.

Don't take the bait to get into an idle religious conversation. We want people to see Jesus. Those who just want to enter a battle about denominations need a factory reset.

Notice that this woman was not a Jew, in the classical sense. Some Christians idolize Israel and so forget the spiritual hunger of the Palestinians and Muslim nations. They talk as if Israel contains the only people of importance in the Middle East.

What if there were more true believers among the Palestinians than the Jews? What if more people in Pakistan and Iran were seeing Jesus Christ than all the Jews in Israel combined? We have to be careful of prejudice today, too.

Notice how Jesus shifted presuppositions. Back when Elder Nick came to Jesus, he probably wanted to have a theological discussion. Instead, Jesus talked about babies being born and the sound the wind makes.

Next, the woman with no theological background came up randomly. With her, Jesus opened deep spiritual insights. Why? She was thirsty. Nick was only curious. Thirsty people draw things out of Jesus.

He said, "Woman, believe Me that an hour is coming when you will worship the Father neither in this mountain nor in

Jerusalem."[172] This woman must realize, as must all humans, that one's location on the planet does not matter. The good news was that soon she and many others would worship the Father from the heart!

Jesus did not speak inclusively to her. He was direct about their religion: "You don't know what you are worshipping."[173] The pop Christian culture of our day would have Jesus tell her, "I know Samaritans have a different path but all paths lead to God." No. He said, "We worship what we know, for salvation is of the Jews."[174]

Jesus was firm on this. Jews were the guardians of the worship to the true God. He, not just humans, ordained worship at His temple in Jerusalem.[175]

But wait, there's more! Jesus had not come to validate Jews but to win them. The Father is no longer pleased with the worship at Jerusalem. He is seeking true worshipers.

God is Spirit.[176] He does not live only in the hills of the Middle East. We cannot physically bow before Him or "kiss His hand" (taking the word "worship" literally). The day has come when we "worship the Father in spirit and in truth."[177]

Some people take Jesus's words to mean spirit OR truth, as if you could choose one or the other to worship the Lord. However, since God is Spirit and also called Spirit of Truth,[178] the two are inseparable. We must find both Spirit and Truth, not either/or.

---

[172] John 4:21, LITV.

[173] See John 4:22.

[174] John 4:22, LITV.

[175] See Deuteronomy 12:5, I Kings 8:29; 14:21.

[176] See John 4:24.

[177] John 4:23, LITV.

[178] See John 16:13.

Like oxygen and hydrogen make water, worship comes from both Spirit and Truth. As you read the Scriptures, certain truths leap out at you. As your eyes open like this, your spirit awakens and you exclaim, "Wow! Thank you, Jesus!" or something similar. Seeing Jesus triggers worship.

Worship, in most cultures, is tied to humanity and lies. Burn incense, walk so many paces, or hang a certain thing in your house. Humans try to appease the unseen forces in many ways. In American culture, some folks use good luck charms to keep away bad things, others celebrate Halloween in an attempt to laugh the evil away, and others use drugs of various types to keep haunting memories away.

Worship is what you do every day, not just during a "worship service." What feet do you kiss all week? The mighty dollar? The power of emotion through love songs or other songs that control how you feel? Do you kiss the feet of sports stars or movie stars? Are you codependent on someone in your life or an enabler for someone you cannot let go?

You must be born of the Spirit to worship in the Spirit. Those not born from above have not seen the Kingdom nor have they truly worshipped, regardless of how large their chest has swelled on the fifth round of "How Great is Our God." Worship is more than a feeling.

Our feelings are the effect we get from praising, singing, and praying. Worship is what God calls our efforts when they are received. I might think I bowed down to kiss His feet when really I'm falling on my face in awe of that singer who just hit three octaves. I could get chill bumps listening to hip-hop or country music (at least in theory). Worship is not measured by whether my spine tingles or I feel happy afterward. The real test is did I touch the King? Did the ultimate Ruler of earth feel moved to hear my voice?

Bowing before a king was about submitting one's self to be a servant to him, to plead a cause, or beg for mercy. Our modern

Christian idea of worship is gently swaying together to a song. True worship happens everywhere for those in whom the Spirit continually leaps up like a fountain. By the Spirit we see the Kingdom, enter the Kingdom, and walk in the continual favor of the King!

The woman at the well now comes closer to worship. She's about to have her eyes opened to Truth and it will change everything about her. Already she had focused on much more important things than just water for survival.

She tells Jesus she knows Messiah was coming and would explain everything.[179] This reference to "Messiah" came mainly from the book of Daniel,[180] a book the Samaritans supposedly did not read! Perhaps she had been digging for truth a little more than the average person.

Of course, as she brought up the Messiah, she watched Him from the corner of her eye to see if He reacted. Her gears were turning. She was wondering if maybe—

"I AM!" Jesus exclaimed.[181]

Most English translations don't say "I AM." They say, "I am He." They insert the word "He" because they assume it should be there, although the original does not contain it.

Jesus is the "I AM," the God who spoke to Moses.[182] This meant a lot to this woman whose culture totally relied on the words of Moses. Later, we will see Jesus emphasize with more clarity that He is the I AM.

Her eyes have been opened. She now must act on what she knows. Her first act of faith is significant, as we will see.

---

[179] See John 4:25.
[180] See Daniel 9:25-26.
[181] John 4:26, LITV.
[182] See Exodus 3:14.

Jesus set the example of how to have a spiritual conversation. He brought the focus to the Lord Himself. He did not get sidetracked in a religious argument (Israel vs. Samaria). He turned that discussion to explain God better.

Jesus did not say things everyone already knew. He spoke in revelations so that eyes would open. Old Nick couldn't have said, "Oh, I know what you are saying about the wind." He was shocked; he'd never heard anything like that before.

The woman had never heard of anyone drinking life-giving water. If we are leaving people bored with worn-out religious expressions, we need to relearn Jesus. She wanted that fountain that would flow into eternity.

Jesus bridged from what she wanted to what she needed. It is not hard to figure out what people need. Telling them what they need tends to make them defensive or dependent on you. We learn to deal with their want (water, for her) to help them get what they need (the Spirit).

Let's look at that principle in business. A chiropractor was not getting many customers, being new in town. So, he brought in a massage therapist and advertised that his office was giving free massages. Though few had come to his office to get their spines adjusted, many began to show up because they simply wanted to feel better after a long day at work. The massage therapist would then mention any spinal issues she detected. "It feels like you have a bulging disc here. Let me call in the doctor to look at it." Suddenly the chiropractor had many new patients. They went from what they wanted to getting what they needed.

In a similar way, we show love, kindness, and friendship to help people at their point of want. Then, as they open up and trust us, they will allow us to help at their point of need. Sharing your own experiences with Jesus can be an effective way of doing this.

COME AND SEE (REMIX)

SO YOU QUIT YOUR JOB and your best friend left his business behind so you could join a dynamic minister who has promised to train you to do great things for God. You love this opportunity to travel and are just learning so much. Then you walk up on your fearless leader one day and find him having a personal conversation alone with the woman everyone in town talks about.

You feel shocked and confused. You want to demand an explanation. Apparently, that's how Jesus's team felt when they walked up on Him and her. I can see one of them dropping the bag with His lunch in it.

They kind of stared at Him, not knowing what to say.[183] Their minds prompted questions like, "What are you after, here?" and "What were you thinking?" Their mouths, fortunately, did not move.

At this point, they were still observing Jesus and probably deciding whether they would commit to follow Him

---

[183] See John 4:27.

permanently. A person wouldn't want to follow a rabbi who had a weak spot for women.

Many male Jews prayed each day, thanking God they were not Gentiles, slaves, nor women. I hate this part of history, but it will help you understand this scene. In this male-dominated culture, women were not human, categorically. Neither were Samaritans. Of course, I would hope none of Jesus's disciples felt this way, but evidences confirm that some did.[184] Thus, they wondered why Jesus would be talking to her.

She walked off the scene. Did the woman feel uncomfortable with the disciples staring at her? Maybe that's why she left. Maybe she wasn't even thinking about them but had to get somewhere to deal with the Truth she had just discovered.

Whatever her motivation for leaving the scene, what she left behind spoke volumes: her water jug.[185] This was not like leaving behind your insulated cup. You needed your water pot for survival.

She must not have worried about leaving her clay jug with Jesus. Do you trust Jesus with your fragile vessel? She knew He provided something better than what her container could hold.

Notice how the switch has flipped, so to speak, inside her. The one who hid from people has been reset as the one who boldly approaches them. Jesus affected her at the core.

She ran to town, telling everyone, "Come, see a Man who told me all things, whatever I did. Is this One not the Christ?"[186]

---

[184] Peter, for example, spoke disrespectfully to some women the night of Jesus's trial, he along with others did not believe the testimony of women who said Jesus had resurrected, and many disciples likewise struggled to accept God's plan for including non-Jews in His Kingdom. These beliefs were deeply ingrained.

[185] See John 4:28.

[186] John 4:29, LITV.

She had figured out what to do with the revelation happening inside her: tell others.

Think back to when Phillip introduced Nathaniel to Jesus. He told him a theological truth: "We have found the One who was prophesied."

But Nate would not take Phillip's word for it.[187] In fact, he challenged him, saying, "Can anything good come out of Nazareth?"

This woman started her conversation where Phillip ended his: "Come and see." She was the underdog in town. They would not have accepted her claims, yet they were willing to come along and check out what she had found.[188]

If you speak and people listen, you have influence. If not, then ask questions to get them to think, to look, to come and see. Like that woman, you do not have to try to tell people all the answers. She simply introduced them to the One who has them.

This woman had become a disciple because this is what disciples do: gather the harvest! She believed into Jesus because she was not afraid of changing her reputation because of Him (Nicodemus was afraid of that). How real is your faith?

Too often, churches expect to make information-experts out of people and then send them out to reap a harvest. She has only known Jesus for an hour or two and she is already telling everyone she knows. Disciples naturally want the people in their social circle to see Jesus.

The Lord's trainees went to town and only brought back bread. She went into town and brought back the hungry. Couldn't the disciples have brought the crowd to Jesus, too?

---

[187] See John 1:44-46.
[188] See John 4:30.

Do you get distracted by details? Life is not about the errands that demand our attention. However, you do not want guilt to drive you to talk to people about Jesus.

Kingdom work cannot be done by our old powers of fear, guilt, and shame. The woman had avoided the people in town probably because of shame. Suddenly, that default reset in the presence of Jesus. Rather than shame governing her interactions with others, compassion drove her to invite them to meet Him.

What drives you on a daily basis? Deadlines and schedules? Obligations and responsibilities? Children and spouse? In your conversations with others are you trying to look good, hide shame, or blend in? What if Jesus reset your defaults?

This story emphasizes for us that there are no "professional" roles of harvesting. We all are harvesters. These who were closest to Jesus did not do so. Of course, they would not have been able to influence the local people the same way the lady at the well could.

While she was busy talking up a crowd in town, the disciples talked to Jesus. "Rabbi, eat!"[189]

Jesus responded, "I have food to eat which you do not know."[190] Jesus had been feasting on something they had never eaten—the Kingdom food. Want a full-filling life? Feast on Kingdom work, bringing people to see Jesus.

Confused, the disciples asked each other, "Has anyone brought Him anything to eat?"[191] They looked around for sandwich wrappers or paper bags. Nothing.

When people do not understand Jesus, it is because they are not close to Him. This is true about understanding Scripture

---

[189] See John 4:31.
[190] John 4:32, LITV.
[191] John 4:33, NKJV.

and following the leading of the Spirit: only those close to Him understand. We should not get upset with people who do not "see" Jesus or His Truth's right away. Misunderstandings are common, but not permanent for the persistent.

With their minds on munchies, they are a little confused when Jesus tells them He's already eaten. This is the second kind of spiritual edibles we learn of from Jesus. First, He had said humans do not live only by bread, but we feast on every word from God's mouth. Now, we learn that one also gets fueled by doing the will of God and completing His work.

Of course, the immediate meaning here is that the Son finds strength in fulfilling the Father's desires. Jesus explained, "My food is that I should do the will of Him who sent Me, and that I may finish His work."[192] By extension, the same is true for His followers. Is that what you feast on?

We find fulfillment and strength in doing the things that please Him. Too many people claim to be believers but do not even know what work He wants them to do. My life would be so empty and unfulfilled if I had not heard the Lord tell me to write and teach for Him.

Sharing the message of hope and discussing spiritual things with others is very fulfilling. I have gone through ministry withdrawal over the holidays at times because I had no one to teach the Bible to. Doing my service in the Kingdom is not just rewarding—it is addicting. Many times while ministering to others, God speaks to me!

How can you have a meaningful life? Don't live for your physical needs. Learn the will of Him who sent you. Then do it. Whether you have money or not, fame or not, comfort or not, your life will have meaning, happiness, and satisfaction.

---

[192] John 4:34, LITV.

BRING IN THE HARVEST

O NE ZEALOUS MAN named Stuart went to a coffee bar downtown to tell young-somethings about Jesus. He got into a conversation with a young coffee drinker who let him open up and talk about Jesus. After listening for a while, the young man finally got up to leave. He told Stuart, "You don't believe a word of all this stuff you've been telling us about God."

Stunned, Stuart asked, "Why would you say that?"

"Because all you have told us here tonight is so wonderful that if you and people like you really believed it, you would have been down here long before tonight to tell us kids about it."[193]

Do we really believe this? Have you forgotten how wonderful Jesus is? Are you really convinced that Jesus is the answer for the lives of everyone you know? Do you believe they cannot make eternity without Him? If we really believed this, wouldn't we talk about it more?

---

[193] Stuart Briscoe, *Flowing Streams*, (Grand Rapids, MI: Zondervan, 2008), 55-56.

The Man at the well had been feasting on doing the will of God. Before one can eat, someone must harvest the food. Jesus now gives them the recipe for being full on the inside: bring in the eternal harvest.

A few months pass between seed planting and harvest time. Jesus probably referenced a common expression in their farming culture when He said, "Do you not say, 'It is yet four months and the harvest comes?'"[194] Farmers would plant the field and then have time to do other things (such as going up to a feast in Jerusalem) until they had to go full-time into harvesting the crop.

Jesus is as good as saying, "This is not like that. No more waiting is necessary. The time for this harvest is now."

He put their attention on something more important than grain, "Lift up your eyes and behold the fields, for they are already white to harvest."[195] Grain blowing in the breeze became sun-bleached when it was ready to cut. If they looked up, they probably saw green blades of grass or green heads of grain at that time of the year. Instead of the white harvest Jesus mentioned.

The ripe harvest is those who are ready for Him. People want to see Jesus right now. Bring them in. Perhaps Jesus looked at the crowd of people coming out of the city with the woman. Maybe He pointed at them as He told the disciples the harvest was ripe! The field is the city, not the empty hills.

As the townspeople swarmed out to meet Jesus, I wonder what the disciples did when they saw the people from Five Guys (or wherever they bought the meal). The people they had just met were now interested in Jesus. I imagine the food vendors looked at the disciples like, "Why didn't you tell us about Him yourself?"

---

[194] John 4:35, LITV, internal quotes added.
[195] John 4:35, LITV.

The disciples were still in observation mode and had not given full commitment to His cause. Jesus was in their prefrontal cortex but not their limbic cortex yet. Meaning, they honored Him in their conscious minds but the Kingdom was not into their subconscious yet. With time, awareness of Him and His Kingdom would sink deep into their impulses and reflexes.

Jesus promised them wages if they became harvesters. He said that the one "who reaps receives wages, and gathers fruit for eternal life."[196] A farmer does not work the field for nothing—it sustains him. Jesus is not asking them to join Him in the cause without taking care of their needs.

Many preachers want to get paid for talking but do not want to bring in the harvest. As the woman was doing at that very moment, all disciples gather the harvest. Many churches today expect paid professional evangelists or polished programs to bring in the lost. If they had more true conversions, publicity would be free.

We have already seen that those who see Jesus and go "all in" with Him will see eternal life. Now, we find how to have fruit in the life that lasts forever—bring in the harvest. Apparently those who become reapers will be taken care of in this life and in the life to come: wages and eternal fruit.

Do you have financial needs? Bring people into the Kingdom. Then watch the Lord take care of your budget!

Jesus explained further, "both the one sowing and the one reaping may rejoice together."[197] Perhaps John had already worked in this area and now that harvest was being reaped. Speaking of the prophets whom the Lord sent to these people, Jesus said, "For in this the saying is true: 'One sows and another

---

[196] John 4:36, NKJV.
[197] John 4:36, LITV.

108

reaps.'"[198] In some people you will plant the seed of the Kingdom; others you will reap into an eternal harvest.

Jesus then said, "I sent you to reap."[199] Wait, what? When did He "send" them?

They were still on the introductory tour. When they were baptizing, He was with them. So that does not count as a true "sending" away from Himself to do His work. Every other event to this point was simply Jesus working miracles and speaking the message while they watched.

Perhaps the only "sending" they had been given to that point was when Jesus sent them into town to grab sandwiches in Sychar. Little did they realize the whole town was ready to meet Jesus. Errands could accomplish something more than you imagined.

Did Jesus think of grabbing lunch as a ministry assignment? Does He intend for us to reach people and reap the harvest as we go about our daily lives? Are you more worried about whether your chicken and onion rings are keto-friendly than if that worker you buy from is in the Kingdom?

Jesus reminds them that they are reaping what they did not labor over (as a farmer plowing, planting, and weeding). He said, "Others have labored, and you have entered into their labor."[200] They had been baptizing disciples whom John had prepared for that moment. Also, as evidenced in the woman's conversation, they were entering into work Moses had done. Later, their mission to Galilee will build on the work begun by Moses, other prophets, and most recently John the Washer.

What is the next Samaria? Where is your Sychar? Is it your next-door neighbor? Refugees in your town?

---

[198] John 4:37, NKJV.
[199] See John 4:38.
[200] John 4:38, LITV.

Jesus is working in your Samaria already, preparing hearts ahead of you. Enter into His labors. Ask Him to show you the ripe harvest.

The teachable moment ended as many came out and "believed into Him, because of the word of the woman."[201] Don't miss the importance of this early moment in Christian history.

A woman had spoken. Her words influenced others to see Jesus and put their lives in His hand. In that culture and time, a woman's voice was not respectable yet Jesus let her carry His message. He still resets social norms like that today.

What prompted her to be so bold? "He told me all things, whatever I did."[202] When Jesus saw who she really was, she saw who He really was.

Many people hesitate to tell others about Jesus because they think they must be highly qualified to do so. This woman did not let her past stop her. Her past motivated her! If none of us needed Jesus, none of us would have come to Him and thus would have no reason to bring others to Him.

That woman was not perfect, but she cared enough to tell others—even those who had gossiped about her, shunned her, and perhaps used her. If a believer is not helping bring others to Jesus it could be one of two causes: a lack of seeing how great Jesus is or a lack of concern for friends without Him.

Comedian and atheist Penn Jillette says he appreciated a man coming up and giving him a Bible and warning him about hellfire. Though he did not convert, he was grateful that the man spoke up for his faith. Jillette said, "How bad do you have to hate someone to believe that everlasting life is possible and not tell

---

[201] John 4:39, LITV.
[202] John 4:39, LITV.

them that?"[203] Yes, how badly must you hate someone to not tell them about the love of Jesus and His power to change a life?

Then, another unusual thing happened: Samaritans invited a Jew to stay in town.[204] He stayed a couple days. The more they got to know Him, the deeper their faith grew.

Soon, they were able to say their faith was not borrowed from anyone but they had heard Jesus for themselves.[205] If we are not careful as parents, ministers, and disciples, we will give people our second-hand faith. They will believe in the Jesus we speak of but never hear His Word for themselves.

Maybe it sounds rude, but they told the woman, "We no longer believe because of your saying; for we ourselves have heard, and we know that this One is truly the Savior of the world, the Christ."[206] As good as your experience with Jesus is, it is not enough for anyone to borrow. Remember the illustration Jesus used with Nicodemus about looking up to the serpent on the pole. No one was saved from poisonous serpents by looking at someone else who looked at the pole—they have to see the One lifted up to be restored.[207]

By telling others about Jesus, we are not just informing or educating them. We call them to action. Birth is dramatic and massively transitional. Saving faith accepts His work and His power in one's life, changing from darkness to light. The gospel demands action and is not just a story to be listened to.

We must be patient with people where they are in the progression toward Jesus. We use wise questions that help awaken their motivation toward Him (everyone is motivated for

---

[203] See personal testimony about this event at
https://www.youtube.com/watch?v=6md638smQd8
[204] See John 4:40.
[205] See John 4:41.
[206] John 4:42, LITV.
[207] See John 3:14-16 to revisit this story.

survival). We use our own stories or tell the experiences of others that help people see Jesus better. Ultimately, they must see Him as "Savior of the world" also and invite Him in to stay.

WHAT THE SPIRIT DOES

THE THIRSTY WOMAN found Living Water in a dusty place between Jerusalem and Galilee. Jesus postponed His trip for two days before proceeding to His motherland.[208] Riding the wave of good reports about Him, Jesus found most people at home welcomed Him back.

Locals came running out to crowd around Jesus as He walked back into Galilee.[209] Many of them had been in Jerusalem and seen the great things He did there. They wanted to see more of Him and find out what else He might do. As He traveled to each town, He taught in their synagogues and became more largely noticed by the people.[210]

Jesus returned to His roots, so to speak, when He went back to Nazareth where He had been brought up.[211] Imagine what was happening in the heads of some of the guys He grew up

---

[208] See Luke 4:14.
[209] See John 4:45.
[210] See Luke 4:15.
[211] See Luke 4:16.

113

with. Did they have a reaction like Nathanael: "Can anything good come out of Nazareth?" Were they surprised when they heard the stories about Him?

In the synagogue, every man would get a turn to read the scrolls. Historical evidence shows that synagogues had a list of reading selections they would use on an assigned schedule. These passages came from the writings of Moses and the prophets.

Jesus, well-accustomed with their routine, chose a different passage. The lectionary lists we have from that time did not include the section He chose. When they handed Him the Isaiah scroll, "He found the place"[212] He wished to read from. He stood and read about the Spirit of the Lord and explained what the Anointing does.

> The Spirit of the Lord is upon Me.
> > Because of this He **anointed** Me
> > > to proclaim the gospel to the poor;
> > He has sent Me
> > > to heal the brokenhearted,
> > > > to proclaim remission to captives,
> > > > and to the blind to see again,
> > > to send away the ones being crushed, in remission,
> > > to preach an acceptable year of the Lord.[213]

The act of "anointing" involved pouring fragrant oil over the head and body of a king, priest, prophet, or someone who had been restored from a deadly disease. Such a pivotal moment marked that person out as dedicated to God, commissioned to serve, or empowered to do the tasks of their assignment.

The many instances of anointing in Hebrew history showed that common people saw the anointed person as distinct from others:

---

[212] Luke 4:17, LITV.
[213] Luke 4:18-19, LITV

- When anointed as king, a man named Jehu tried to play it off as no big deal. Realizing what this meant, his fellow captains suddenly threw down their robes and set him on them at the top of the staircase to honor him in his new role.[214]
- When anointed to speak for God, a farmer named Elisha left his trade and consumed himself with developing his new purpose as a prophet.[215]
- When anointed as priest, Moses's brother Aaron felt the oil soak through his hair, into his beard, and down through his clothes until it dripped from the hem.[216]
- A person with a highly contagious skin disease would have to stay away from everyone else until cured. Once such a body healed, a Hebrew priest would anoint it with oil, marking the person as safe for society.[217]

Jesus came back to Galilee anointed with the "power of the Spirit."[218]

At His baptism, He was full of the Spirit and in the wilderness led of the Spirit.[219] He never needed a factory reset because He is the factory original, but now, with the Spirit in full power, Jesus stood out. He was the only human functioning under original factory specs. People couldn't help but notice the different operating system and began to crowd around Him.

Most minds of the time associated anointing oil with the authorization of a king. A prophet anointed a man named Saul as the first king of Israel. King Saul's morals and mental stability went to the swamp in short order. God chose David to replace Saul and had the prophet Samuel anoint him king in Saul's place.

---

214 See II Kings 9:11-13.

215 See I Kings 19:19-21.

216 See Exodus 29:4-7; Leviticus 8:12; Psalm 133:2.

217 See Leviticus 14:15-18.

218 Luke 4:14, LITV.

219 See Luke 4:1.

Saul still had the throne and tried to kill David. Even though Saul became driven by an evil spirit, David still referred to him as the "Lord's Anointed."

In fact, when David called him that, he literally said, "The Lord's Messiah." Yes, both David and Saul were called "messiah," which simply means 'anointed.'[220] Therefore, when the Jewish people spoke of the coming Messiah, they were speaking of a special King, like David, who would save them from the oppressive nations around them. The word "Messiah" referred specifically to the King.

Greek speakers translated "Messiah" to *christos*, 'the Anointed,' from which we get the word "Christ." Thus, when we say, "Jesus Christ" we are actually referring to "Jesus the Anointed." Practically, then, this means "Jesus the King." To recognize Jesus as Messiah, as the woman at the well and her neighbors did, was to see Him as the ultimate King.

Now, you can see why Jesus could not be too public with His identity until it was time for Him to die. To be King, He would take power from the existing magistrates. Rulers in that time killed their competitors.

In the immediate sense, believing on Jesus as Messiah/King was to submit to Him as commander in your life. Jews have an ancient blessing that says, "Blessed are You, Lord our God, King of the universe." They knew that Yahweh is King of everything. To see Jesus as King was to accept Him as Lord of heaven and earth: God in flesh!

Samuel anointed Saul and David as kings of Israel, but who anointed Jesus the King? Elijah anointed Elisha the prophet, but who anointed the Prophet? Jesus explains this

---

[220] See I Samuel 24:6; 26:9; II Samuel 22:51; 23:1. The Hebrew word here is *mâshıyach*.

Himself: "The Spirit of the Lord is upon Me. Because of this He anointed Me."[221]

Luke told us how dramatically that anointing took place: the Spirit appeared as a dove coming down upon Him. Instead of being anointed by a human, Jesus was anointed by the highest Source. If a prophet of Israel had anointed Him, He might be king of Israel. If Moses had anointed Him, He would have been priest of Israel. Anointed from above, Jesus is the Prophet to the whole earth, Priest to all humanity, and King of the universe.

Once again, Jesus used what people understood to illustrate what was "out of this world." A joyful wedding, birth of a child, living water, and now a royal anointing. Each of these scenes showed them what the Spirit is like. Those who believe into Him share in His wine/birth/fountain/anointing from above! The Spirit empowers His "anointed ones,"[222] to do these tasks!

If Jesus is King, then He has authority over something. What does He command? What changes does His administration make? He explains:

He has anointed Me to proclaim the gospel to the poor[223]
Jesus brought good news to those without hope in this world. People with lots of money and possessions might be too satisfied to see Jesus. Those in poverty often see Jesus faster because they are looking for hope.

Are you poor or satisfied with your junk? What is your security? Investments, retirement, job, possessions? A little piece

---

[221] Luke 4:18, LITV.

[222] See I John 2:20, 27. We have an anointing, χρίσμα, "*chrisma,*" which comes from the same root as "Christ," Χριστός "*Christos,*" the Anointed One! Furthermore, the root of the word "Christian," Χριστιανός "*Christianos,*" signifies that we are the "anointed ones"! In a much later book, we will examine how Christ lives through us.

[223] Luke 4:18, LITV.

could fall out of place and your "security" would be lost. If you make more than $60 per week, you have it better than half the people on earth.[224] We should be overwhelmed with gratitude for anything we own rather than continually reaching for more.

"To preach the gospel to the poor"[225] is not a pulpit-to-pew exercise. This is a life-giving announcement in any location where an audience will listen. Many people today are relationally poor. They have lived through broken or manipulative relationships and find themselves craving true friendship. The followers of Jesus fill those needs and bring them to Jesus, the best Friend.

He has sent Me to heal the brokenhearted[226]
Jesus heals broken hearts like the one He met at the well. Heartbreak can come from situations that bring sorrow.[227] Even the rich and religious need help in this area.

While many Christians make a lot of noise about sharing the Gospel, too many are silent on healing the brokenhearted. Sometimes this core element must happen before outsiders will receive the Good News of the Kingdom. I believe this is a true physical healing that takes place in the amygdala and the limbic cortex.

Your heart, or the center of your emotions, should function in a healthy way. Living in fear will destabilize you worse than walking on a broken leg. Being triggered by rage is like trying to heat your home with a dumpster fire; yes it produces heat, but the toxic effects of that power is killing you and those you love. Letting guilt drive your actions will sever friendships and sear kindness from your soul.

---

[224] A Gallop poll in 2013 showed per capita median income at less than $3,000 per year.

[225] Luke 4:18, NKJV.

[226] Luke 4:18, LITV.

[227] See Proverbs 15:14.

Nearly every adult and too many children have been scarred or broken in life. Only the King from above can transform something mangled into something beautiful. Let Him miraculously transform you to the core. If you have entered the factory reset, the Lord will send you to hurting people with His power working through you to heal them.

To proclaim remission to captives[228]

Captives, or prisoners of war, have been pinned down by temptations in life. Everyone has been taken hostage by sin. Everyone needs deliverance.

Through King Jesus, we can "proclaim liberty to the captives"![229] You become an agent of the King and give them the hope for freedom! His power snaps the chains of addictions to drugs, sex, money, food, and much more.

Alcohol, marijuana, cocaine, and many other forces held a man named Jeff captive. When Jesus filled him with His Spirit, He broke those powers! Jeff Ready later went to a Bible college and is now a traveling minister helping believers reach other cultures.

Patricia had smoked every day since she was 16 years old. One day in her 30's, the Spirit of the Lord came upon her. She went home afterward and tried to smoke a cigarette. She got sick and nearly vomited. She never smoked again nor did she have any more desire to smoke.

Addictions are not behavioral issues. An addiction, like most habits, gets deep into the subconscious, chemical-driven, automatically triggered part of the brain. This is why people can think about their addictions and talk about them in such a way that they decide to not continue, yet their body impulsively goes back to them. Jesus came to set us from this internal trap, to get us out of that endless loop.

---

[228] Luke 4:18, LITV.
[229] Luke 4:18, NKJV.

And to the blind to see again[230]

People are born spiritually blind. To see Jesus, their eyes must open. The Anointed One brought "recovery of sight to the blind."[231] He would literally heal physical eyes that could not see.

Like all of His miracles, opening blinded eyes demonstrated the Kingdom. The King opens spiritual eyes so we can see Him and His purposes. Everyone needs this internal miracle.

Notice the spiritual progression like a child's eyesight developing. First, people see Jesus but do not really perceive what they are looking at. Next, they begin to glimpse things about Him that bring them excitement and hope. As they follow Him into the Kingdom, they begin to see not only the King but the whole realm of His influence and how it changes everything. Your eyes will continually open to see more of the Kingdom once you are born into it.

To send away the ones being crushed, in remission[232]

Those who are overloaded have no freedom. The King sets "at liberty those who are oppressed." As you will see in this lesson and multiple other times, Jesus set demonized hostages free and sent them out in freedom.

This kind of power in a person's life goes beyond the physical. Some addictions and choices a person makes open the door to forces that science cannot explain. More than a reset, the remedy for these evil presences in a person's life is complete removal.

There is no reset for a demon. They cannot be salvaged, forgiven, or saved. Humans are not compatible with the forces of darkness.

---

[230] Luke 4:18, LITV.

[231] Luke 4:18, NKJV.

[232] Luke 4:18, LITV.

Demons swarm through the world. They have one agenda: to doom humans to their same eternal fate. Like disease to the human body, these spiritual pathogens attack the weak spots in the human spirit. They can use anger, selfishness, pride, and greed as doors of access to rule a human's thinking and actions.

Evil spirits can only work with those whose wills and desires give them a place to hang on. In the King's realm, demons have no power. When a person aligns his or her will with the King's desires, the demons must go. Jesus works through Spirit-filled believers today to also throw out demons with just a command!

To preach an acceptable year of the Lord[233]

People live under fear of doom. Guilt gives you an awareness of your need for punishment for wrongs you have done. The Anointed One did not come to condemn us but to bring us into the favor of the Judge. He announces the era of God's favor: the "year" of the Lord's acceptance!

The Spirit brings hope. Right now is the time to declare God's gracious favor! Jesus omitted the statement "the day of vengeance of our God" from the passage He read in Isaiah.[234] You are living in the realm of the Anointed, a time when people can be soaked with God's Spirit. The wrath and vengeance of God will come once this era ends.

Shame drives some people to try to please God. Others live in fear of Him striking at them. They might feel He is angry at them for bad things they did in the past. What a joy to discover that we live in the time of God's favor and acceptance! This does not mean He just tolerates us but that He approves of those who turn to Him! God is cheering for you!

As a child, I got to spend time with a young man named Timothy Heard. He was a few years older than me, so we didn't

---

233 Luke 4:19, LITV.

234 See Isaiah 61:1-2.

really hang together much. But, he was a good skateboarder and I was learning how to skateboard at the time, so I looked up to him. Little did I know what was happening in the life of this young man whose dad pastored a large church near Toronto.

Tim could claim that he had been born of water and Spirit. He grew up hearing the Bible inside and out, yet he had fallen into the wrong crowd. At the various times I saw him through my teen years, I saw he could fit in with the church crowd as well as with the skateboarders who weren't so religious.

By the time I had met him, Tim was already using nicotine, alcohol, and marijuana (though I didn't know this at the time). By age eighteen, he discovered cocaine, LSD, and psychedelic mushrooms. By his early thirties, crack cocaine took his life for another drastic downturn. His addiction left him incarcerated several times, divorced after a three-week marriage, and defrocked from his Canadian citizenship, to name a few effects of his being held captive. Though he tried going clean and entering programs, he relapsed time and again.

Finally, in his early forties, Timothy hit the factory reset. Another program, another church, more accountability partners. This time, though, he woke to the fact that he did not have the power within himself to do life. Though he had experienced the Spirit of the Lord within him before, this time the Spirit birthed something new in him.

Open eyes and vulnerable heart, something changed at the core of his being. He realized he needed God 100%, not just as an attachment to help with drug issues. Since then, he has put down deep roots, surrendered everything to Jesus, and let Him run his life. The Lord is working through Timothy Heard to set other captives free from a life of substance abuse.[235]

---

[235] Timothy Heard hosts an encouragement page for those in recovery at Facebook.com/#!/RKVRYWRKZ/ and can be contacted to speak to your church or group.

A CLOSED BOOK

AN OLD MAN STOOD in the crowded Nazareth synagogue stroking his beard, staring intently at the young Man reading out loud. The crowd watched with admiration as one of their own spoke with flowing words. "There is something about him," they thought as they watched Him roll up the scroll and hand it to the custodian.[236]

He said, "Today this Scripture has been fulfilled in your ears."[237] This was heavy stuff. They had longed for their King. They knew a great day was coming, but it was always so far away that it had become just a legend.

Now? Today? Hmm.

"That's Joseph's boy," one man said to an elderly gent.[238]

"I can tell that," said another, "but I still don't believe it."

---

[236] See Luke 4:20.
[237] Luke 4:21, LITV.
[238] See Luke 4:22.

Jesus sat down in "Moses's seat," as they called the teacher's chair, and looked into their eyes. The prophecy of the King and Kingdom was unfolding before them. Instead of seeing Him, they only saw Joseph's boy.

It was their custom to be here, just as it was His. Yet He was moving forward according to the plan written in those old scrolls. They lived by their custom of unrolling those promises and then wrapping them back up, week after week.

John had said the chosen One would baptize with the Spirit. Jesus had just declared, "The Spirit is upon Me!" Did they nod in agreement? Or did they nod off?

This same Spirit will wake you up at night to pray for someone. He will put words in your mouth for you to say to help heal a broken heart. This Anointing works through us to open eyes and set prisoners free from what has bound them. The King in us gives us authority over the evil forces.

Yet His own people sat there and stared. Many Christians today—Jesus's own people—blink and listen to the repetition of words and phrases about the Spirit without understanding the power within their reach. Their very religious lives are still thirsty and they do not know Him as the fountain.

Jesus did not commit Himself to His homies; He knew what is in them. He knew humans would welcome a stranger faster than one of their own. You might face the same rejection from your own close family members because "a prophet has no honor in his own fatherland."[239]

He knew they would one day mock Him. They would yell at Him on the cross: "Doctor, heal yourself." They did not believe. "What things we heard"[240] is not the same as them

---

239 John 4:44, LITV. This verse appears to be John's quick summary of this whole encounter. See also Luke 4:24.
240 Luke 4:23, LITV.

believing the reports about what He had done. They would challenge Him to perform for their skeptical eyes.

From Capernaum, Jesus would launch His new Kingdom order. To this point, the narrative has not mentioned any miracles happening in Capernaum. Jesus tells them in advance what He would do as well as how they would respond to it.

Well, this isn't the way to win friends and get your best life now! What happened to Jesus's public speaking skills? Did He skip a point in His three-point sermon?

Preaching is not intended to get people to hate you. There was no hate in His voice, but there was in their eyes. How sad He must have felt to see so many familiar faces who would soon disown Him.

How soon would things fall apart? In at least three and a half years. That's the length of the drought during the time Elijah ministered. He was a mighty prophet among the people of Israel, but they had become so caught up in other things, they weren't interested in the message from above.

Jesus spoke these words in the northern parts of Israel, near where Elijah prophesied as well. After telling Israel's king that it would not rain until he said so, Elijah left the hostile scene. While Jesus could have spoken about many aspects in Elijah's ministry similar to His own, He focused on this divisive issue: Elijah had to work outside his homeland.

It's not like there were no needs among the people whom God claimed. In all honesty, Jesus explained, "Many widows were in Israel in the days of Elijah when the heaven was shut up over three years and six months, when a great famine came on all the land."[241] Then, to make His case, Jesus explained, "Elijah was sent to none of them except to Zarephath of Sidon, to a widow

---

[241] Luke 4:25, LITV.

woman."[242] He worked a miracle so she would always have bread to eat.

His hometown peeps didn't want to hear that. A woman? A widow? A heathen? If that overlooked person received the great miracle worker, what would come of Nazareth? They would refuse the reset.

Jesus had just suggested that the Lord was going to go around them and reach insignificant others. These people would not see the greatness before them and would miss their moment. This had happened in Samaria. What would the Nazarenes think if they knew about the hated woman who called Him "Messiah"?

Remember that provision in the Law about anointing the person healed of some form of a highly contagious skin disease? No one in Israel ever was healed. At least we don't have a story of a Hebrew being cured of leprosy.

However, through the prophet Elisha a leper (a person with that terrible skin disease) received a miraculous healing. That man, named Naaman, was from the neighboring country of Syria.[243] Like Elisha, Jesus would have much honor outside His own town and away from His own family.

Many preachers today appeal for people to come forward after they preach. Jesus's sermon ended with people coming forward—to carry Him out! Angry people moved blindly, grabbing the Man they could not see.[244] Pushing Him to the edge of the city's hill, they wanted to toss Him sixty feet to the rocks below.[245]

---

[242] Luke 4:26, LITV. See that story in I Kings 17:1-24; 18:1-2.

[243] See Luke 4:27 and II Kings 5:1-27.

[244] See Luke 4:28.

[245] See Luke 4:29.

"He went away, passing through their midst."[246] How did He get away? Probably because they could not see Him. They never had. Their religion blinded them.

Jesus did not play by their rules. He identified Himself outside of them rather than as them. When you choose to identify with Jesus instead of your religious circle, you will get pushed, too!

Religion so easily blinds us. Religious devotees do not see Him correctly. Perhaps we seek an "atta-boy" Jesus who performs as we expect.

Perhaps we are not seeing the true Jesus because our preconceptions are speaking so loudly. Who is more likely to miss Jesus: someone who has never met Him before or someone who has grown up around Him? Being familiar with a Jesus-religion puts us in danger of not truly seeing Him.

They dragged Jesus out of church to kill Him. It was the acceptable year of the Lord, yet the Lord was not accepted. As an expert communicator, Jesus may have incited this response to detached Himself from His people. Otherwise, they might have claimed Him without following Him, confusing what others understood about Him. He did not seek admirers but disciples.

Jesus gets this same treatment in denominations today. It is easier to reach people for Jesus outside of churches than in them because religious people are saying, "There's our boy!" Yet they do not hear Him or let Him live through them.

Jesus had crowds talking for Him, telling others what He meant. Who actually listens to Him? Who truly sees Him and not only what they want to see?

Like then, people today make rituals to protect the things of God. The rituals take on their own life and obscure God's own

---

[246] Luke 4:30, LITV.

plan. People in Iran and China find the true Jesus easier than churches in free countries do. Some people in the jail cells are hungrier than many church attenders.

Let me give you an illustration of a person being blind to Jesus. One traveling preacher said his records showed that 80% of people healed at their events came from no religion or dead religion. The least likely to be healed were Pentecostals and Charismatics. Too many Spirit-filled denominations have seen people prayed for who did not get healed. Then came a doctrine of, "You have to wait and see if it is God's will to heal." Jesus healed all that had need.

Are you so used to the patented thing that you will miss the powerful thing? It does not matter what school you went to or how many years you have invested in your religion, you have to get this from the core. It will not be enough for you to get Christianity 2.0. It is not enough to find a better denomination. If you truly see Jesus, everything about your life will change.

Jesus is more than a three-step plan or a twelve-step tradition. This is about you being born as a new creature and getting a new way of thinking. The Spirit of the Lord causes the factory reset within us! The very life and identity of Jesus will live through a person.

AT HIS WORD

AFTER ESCAPING NAZARETH with His life, Jesus continued toward Capernaum. There He would officially launch His Kingdom campaign. On the way, He went through a town called Cana.[247] There, His disciples had first seen His miracle power at the wedding feast only a few months before.

A government official in Capernaum happened to hear that Jesus had come back to Galilee. The news of the riot in Nazareth traveled a long way, but even bad news is free publicity. The man's son was dying and he could not waste time waiting.

The nobleman left his home in Capernaum and hurried to find Jesus. Catching Him in Cana, the man dropped all his dignity and begged Jesus to help.[248] This official worked for Herod Antipas, most likely. That would mean his boss was the same dude who imprisoned John.

The official had not come to split hairs with Jesus about how He interpreted Isaiah chapter 61. He simply knew he needed Jesus to heal his home. Maybe you are like that. You don't really

---

[247] See John 4:46.
[248] See John 4:47.

care about all the fancy religious debates but just want Jesus in your home.

Jesus responded abruptly to the pleading father: "Unless you people see signs and wonders, you will by no means believe."[249] Jesus's statement seems lost on this man. It does not appear he was struggling with accepting Jesus as King of Israel or not. He just wanted his son to live and there was not much time. The man had focused on the crisis at hand—any miracle-worker would do.

An employer at an interview says to the applicant, "You say you can do web design. Do you have any examples of your work?" It is right for a prospective boss to look for a sign or evidence that you are capable before he hires you. Similarly, Jesus was being "checked out." It was not enough for Him to proclaim Himself as Messiah. People wanted to see proof.

We do not need proof to believe into Jesus as King of all. Whether we perceive it or not, He is true. Because of weak faith and spiritual blindness, people cannot see Him unless something dramatic turns their heads.

The man became demanding with Jesus. He switched from his begging voice to his official tone: "Come down before my child dies."[250] He was used to bossing people around. Except for the "sir" part, that was how he would have given orders to his underlings. Literally, he said, "You, come now!"

Jesus had not applied for this job. An assistant manager takes orders from the manager, but the CEO does not have to do what the janitor commands. Jesus will not be pushed around by Mr. Fancy Pants. He has an order of His own for the man: "You, go now!"

---

[249] John 4:48, NKJV.
[250] See John 4:49, LITV.

To the man who as much as said, "Come, now!" Jesus responded, "Go! Your son lives."[251] Jesus outranks the king's official. Being a minion of Herod was nothing compared to being King of the Universe.

That man was used to giving orders, but in that moment he was desperate enough to take them. He believed Jesus. There was something solid in His words, and the official put his roots into them.

Capernaum, where the man's son lived, lay thirty miles to the north of Cana, which was only a few miles away from Nazareth. So why does the text say the man went "down" from Cana? Because Capernaum was on the coast of the Sea of Galilee and thus was much lower in elevation than Cana in the hill land.[252]

Since a twenty-miles-plus journey took many hours, the man did not hear word from home until the next day. Meeting up with his servants halfway, the man heard the confirmation of what he had believed, "Your child lives."[253] He was right to put his trust in Jesus.

Then, as quickly as he could process this good news, he had to ask, "When? When did it happen?" You can see the childish joy and excitement spreading on his face. He had heard of such things but never experienced them. How did this thing work? How quickly did He do it?

"Yesterday at one o'clock," they said.[254]

---

[251] John 4:50, LITV.

[252] Furthermore, "going down" would not be how they thought of a southern destination. We think of north as being "up." To the eastern mind, the east was like the top of the compass, not the north.

[253] John 4:51, LITV.

[254] See John 4:52. The "seventh hour" in the text refers to their method of counting hours from daylight (around 6 am). Seven hours past six in the morning would be one in the afternoon.

The nobleman's face could not hide it. Joy tugged at the corners of his mouth until a full smile emerged. His face radiated with such happiness that his smile almost eclipsed his eyes, and then a laugh broke out. "Immediately!" he may have exclaimed. "Jesus did it immediately!"

Then, just as quickly a deeper feeling tugged at his heart. "Jesus is the One," it said. There was no unconvincing him now. Or his family. They all were raving fans of Jesus.[255] Just think, He was on the way to their town next!

According to missionary Mark Shutes, "signs" cause people to believe and "wonders" break the power of the enemy. The first sign in Cana was Jesus removed the shame of a bride and groom who had not planned well and revealed how He brings something better than anything before Him. The second sign[256] revealed the true King to an official of the current "king."

Did the disciples see this sign? At the first miracle in Cana, Jesus's disciples believed on Him. Why are they not mentioned in the second sign in Cana?

Did you notice the disciples were not mentioned also in the recent scuffle in Nazareth? If the people were trying to push Jesus off a cliff, where were His followers? It they had been with Him, wouldn't they have defended Him or gotten pushed, too? That story and the one in Cana mention Jesus alone.

Something happened after Samaria. Jesus stayed for two days. Did His followers? For some Jews, it would have been too much to see Him talking with a woman. Some Jews would have run from the idea of Jesus staying with the Samaritans, eating their food and sleeping in their homes.

I'm not saying Jesus's disciples forsook Him at this point. According to Bill Hull, the encounter in Sychar signaled an end

---

[255] See John 4:53.
[256] See John 4:54.

to their first tour with Jesus. It only lasted a few months and required no solid commitment from them.[257] They simply traveled with Jesus, learned from Him, and observed what was happening.

Jesus's impassioned speech for them to consider working with Him in the ripened fields may have also been a goodbye speech. Not "goodbye forever," but "goodbye for now and think about this while we are apart" kind of thing.

After they took a break before His big launch in Capernaum, they had some time to think about what He said. While hauling fish onto the boat, James and John thought about that harvest. Peter and Andrew talked about what Jesus meant when He said they would receive wages for gathering a Kingdom harvest.

Are you in such a time of reflection? You have followed Jesus a certain distance. You've seen the signs that caused you to believe, but how deeply has that changed you? Is He calling you to the harvest?

---

[257] Bill Hull. *Jesus Christ, Disciple Maker*, (Grand Rapids, MI: Revell, 1984).

TO THOSE IN RECOVERY

YOU'VE BEEN REJECTED. Wasn't it great? Oh, I know it feels horrible to have people you care about "throw you under the bus," but think about some of the rejection we have seen so far.

While Jesus and His team were baptizing, one of the few people who understood Him got arrested. As you may recall, John went to the dungeon for speaking out against the immorality of Herod, the so-called king. Perhaps you have done the right thing before only to get smacked down for it. John knew Jesus should be King and Herod Antipas's actions disqualified him from such a title. Perhaps John even called for Herod's removal because of his immorality.

Jesus came to harvest what John had planted. Since the hard soils of Nazareth did not produce a yield, Jesus quickly moved on. In Cana, He crossed paths with a man who became a believer, but Jesus wasn't stopping there. The faith may have been in Cana, but the miracle happened in Capernaum.

Jesus's rejection in Nazareth fulfilled prophecy. In other words, that hurtful experience lined up with God's foreseen predictions. Remember, His birth only happened in Bethlehem because of hateful circumstances, yet it was God's perfect will. What is God birthing in you through rejection, confusion, and hateful people?

His move to Capernaum fulfilled another prophecy. "He lived at Capernaum, beside the sea in the districts of Zebulun and Naphtali."[258] When the tribes of Israel first filled the Promised Land, Zebulun's tribe took the region of Lower Galilee and Naphtali filled Upper Galilee. Isaiah called the region, "Galilee of the Gentiles"[259] because Gentiles (non-Jews) lived in that area even after Israel took the land.

Why were these people living outside the covenant yet benefiting from it? First, the Hebrews never fully drove out the Gentile presence here, as they were told to do.[260] Plus, Solomon gave Galilean cities to a Gentile king named Hiram.[261] Later, it was the first area to fall when Assyria invaded.[262]

Many of Jesus's disciples were from this region. Philip and Andrew were both from Galilee and their names were not of Hebrew origin. While they were most likely Hebrew in ancestry, their names indicate the mixed influences if not also mixed ethnicity in the area.

Jesus likes to work in a multiethnic mix. His own family tree includes many from outside the chosen gene pool. Missionary Robert Dame tells how he has noticed during his travels that the churches with a mix of multicultural members have a greater presence of Jesus.

The Lord set up His headquarters in the midst of a strong and loyal Jewish population coexisting alongside Gentile

---

258 Matthew 4:13, LITV.

259 See Isaiah 9:1 and Matthew 4:14-15.

260 See Judges 1:30, 33.

261 See I Kings 9:11.

262 See II Kings 15:29.

genetics. The King would not rule from Jerusalem, the center of human power struggles in the nation. He would come to the underdogs in an uncelebrated population.

Jesus came to people in recovery. People like you and me: "the people sitting in darkness saw a great Light; and to those sitting in the region and shadow of death, Light sprang up to them."[263]

Galilee sat in the valley of the shadow of death.[264] The nobleman from Capernaum first saw the Light. This "Light" Isaiah spoke of is the Child who has been born, the Son who was given.[265] Those who look, see Jesus as the Counselor of wonder, the Prince of peace, the God of might, and the Father of eternity.[266] Those opting for His reset let Him shoulder the management of their lives, become King on their heart's throne, ruling forever with peace and justice.[267]

You cannot have a kingdom without a king. John had already announced the coming of this Kingdom. Jesus followed close behind, announcing the good news of the Kingdom.[268]

Typically, this is called the "Kingdom of God."[269] The Gospel of Matthew more often uses the phrase "Kingdom of Heaven."[270] Many Jews substituted the word "heaven" for "God" so that they did not carelessly use His name. Sadly, modern assumptions about Heaven give readers the wrong impression about what this phrase means.

---

[263] Matthew 4:16, LITV. See also Isaiah 9:2.

[264] See Psalm 23:4 with Isaiah 9:2.

[265] See Isaiah 9:6.

[266] See Isaiah 9:7.

[267] See Isaiah 9:7.

[268] See Mark 1:14; Luke 4:31.

[269] See Mark 1:14.

[270] See Matthew 4:17.

Heaven is the unseen eternal realm, the origin of the Kingdom. God is the King of that realm. The word for "Heaven" is also the word for the sky.[271] Imagine someone marching into your town shouting, "Change your lives because the Kingdom of the Sky is almost here!"

Wait, shouldn't a preacher in Israel talk about the Kingdom of Israel? Shouldn't He have used those corporate catchphrases many churches now use? "This is going to be our best year yet." And, "Hang in there, Israel, God's not done with you." Or "We are going to get this thing turned around and be even better with our five-year initiative!"

Yeah, Jesus didn't come with a bunch of hype. He wasn't trying to improve the existing system. He was replacing it.

Imagine a person shouting in a shopping mall in the United States, "Get ready, a new nation is beginning! This won't be Republican or Democrat! It won't be a nation like any you have ever known before. It will be a new kingdom with a great king!" Sound crazy? You would have to change your thinking to align with this new cause.

To religious people longing for a new and more powerful Kingdom of Israel, Jesus commanded them to turn and change their ways and thinking. They would have to turn from thinking that their self-improvements were valid. Their perfecting of the rules and making new ones would not count for anything in the new Kingdom.

John came preparing the people for the new King. Now, the King comes announcing His Kingdom, though most do not

---

[271] From the Greek word *"ouranos"* referring to the place above or elevated. While it might be confusing to the Western mind to think of one word referencing both the sky and Heaven, there was a graduation of this term: the first heaven is what we would think of as sky or atmosphere, the second heaven would be outer space with stars and moon, and the third heaven would be the realm where God ruled from high above all else.

know His identity. They will have to discover who the King is as they come close to Him.

Without drawing direct attention to Himself as this King, Jesus went into Galilee announcing, "The time is fulfilled, and the Kingdom of God is at hand!"[272] For there to be a kingdom, there must be a king. The Kingdom is at hand because the King is within reach.

Jesus said, "Repent!"[273]

Too often, modern Christians think of "repent" as a message to wicked people. Jesus had to tell the religious to repent. Their ways, methods, and programs were the problem, keeping most from seeing Him and His Kingdom.

Manmade methods, experiential doctrines, and peer expectations bog down many religions. A new operating system has arrived. Will you take the reset?

"Repent!"

Will Jesus become how you process everything? Or were you just looking for an update to validate your already established beliefs and practices?

Has Jesus changed you to the very core? Or did you just get an emotional boost from Him at some point? Which of your religious assumptions has He destroyed? Name some dead ruts you turned away from as He opened your eyes to the shadow of death over your actions and practices.

As we continue through this series, you will see Jesus marching into your life. He will point to some areas you had never thought twice about. He will speak to you about specific

---

[272] Mark 1:15, NKJV.
[273] Matthew 4:17, LITV.

things He wants you to let go of, things you need to pick up, and desires you must let Him transform.

Your understanding of His Kingdom will grow as you make these changes. Each time you turn because of what you see of Jesus, the more you will face Him and the better you will see Him.

"Repent!"

FORSAKE ALL

THE EARLY MORNING SKY lit up the coast of the Sea of Galilee (also called "Lake Gennesaret") on the west side, near the city of Capernaum. Jesus saw two docked fishing boats and workers cleaning and repairing the big nets. Simon and Andrew were still trying to catch something with small nets they were tossing along the shore.[274]

Jesus had come into the area preaching the exciting news about the Nation of God. Hearing His call to turn and embrace this new life, the people of Capernaum crowded around to hear more.[275] The crowds were smushing Jesus into the water.

He decided to use the best public amplification system of the day: speaking from a boat across calm water. Jesus had climbed into the boat of Simon, a.k.a. "The Rock," and made

---

[274] The difference between the Greek word for "net" in Mark 1:16 and the one used in Luke 5:2 show the difference in types. In Mark 1:16 and Matthew 4:18, Peter and Andrew were using the shallow-water kind, while in the Luke 5 story, they used the deep-water kind between two boats.

[275] See Luke 5:1.

Himself comfortable.[276] Hundreds could crowd onto the shoreline and hear Him tell of the Kingdom.

Do people want to hear from God today? Yes, but social media trains us to listen to the crowd instead of the crowd hushing to hear from Jesus. Are you pressing closer to Jesus? Or do you feel you have the Kingdom of the Sky all figured out?

Jesus did more than just yell "Repent!" He began to teach them. If they were going to enter the Nation-From-Above they had to learn more about it.

The crowds on the shore needed to learn, and so did the disciples. Peter, Andrew, James, John, and the others had gone back to work. A few months have passed since Samaria.

Now, Jesus was back in Capernaum. The official launch had begun. Many of His disciples lived in this area and harvested fish for a living.

When Jesus finished speaking to the people, it was time to teach the disciples an unforgettable lesson. "Launch out into the deep and let down your nets for a catch."[277] Hang on, Rabbi, there's something you should know.

Simon, also known as "Peter" or "Rocky," had not interrupted Jesus throughout His teaching. That just was not his place. But now, he had a thing or two to say about fishing.

"Master, laboring all through the night we took nothing."[278] They ran their fishing operation at night because the heat of the day would push the fish too deep for their nets to grab them. The morning market paid well for fish caught fresh just a few hours before.

---

[276] See Luke 5:3.
[277] Luke 5:4, NKJV.
[278] Luke 5:5, LITV.

Simon explained to Jesus that last night's fishing operation was a bust. If the fish were nowhere to be found at night, they certainly won't be easy to grab now that the sun was up. The workers were worn out and probably just ready to go get some sleep.

Jesus didn't drop His gaze. Rocky knew Him well enough now to know that look. Something moved deep within him. That miracle at the wedding feast had retuned his assumptions of what was "impossible."

Knowing that Jesus had a lot more that Peter did not comprehend, he gave Jesus the benefit of the belief. "However," Simon said while glancing from His face to the surface of the water, "at Your word, I will let down the net."[279]

Simon was just playing along. In a real fishing operation, both fishing boats would have been out on the water. They would stretch the net between them. The top side of the net had floats on it. The bottom had weights. Holding both ends of the net from either ship, they would troll forward and scoop up schools of fish.

The fisherman tossed the net out from his solitary boat. While he lashed down the second rope, it suddenly went from lazily dangling in the water to being so tight the boat began to rock. Shaking inside, Rocky looked into Jesus's smiling face. The net was so full it began to rip and the force could capsize the boat.[280]

Quickly, Simon and Andrew hollered to James and John to bring their ship out. Only by their years of experience were the two teams able to untie the second end of the net from Simon's boat and lock it down on Zebedee's. Both ships struggled to bring the fish to land—nearly sinking in the process.[281]

---

[279] Luke 5:5, LITV.

[280] See Luke 5:6.

[281] See Luke 5:7.

142

Simon had just tried to school Jesus on fish. Now, Pete became the student again. This miracle hit much closer to home for him than the wedding beverage incident.

Rocky knew fish; they were his life. He knew how fish thought and how the lake worked. Jesus had just changed something Simon Peter knew was impossible.

If Jesus had power over something so close to the Rockstar's heart, He had to know everything. Overwhelmed, he worshiped Jesus, saying, "Depart from me, for I am a sinful man, Lord."[282]

The Rock crumbled. It was not so much the challenge of getting the fish to shore. It wasn't so much the danger of sinking. It was the shock that Jesus could do something right under his feet.

Clearly, he had not thought through his words, "Get away from me!" Where was Jesus supposed to "go away" while in the middle of the lake? For a reason Jesus had dubbed this unstable and easily overwhelmed man, "the Rock."

Peter caught a glimpse of Jesus in a way that made him ashamed of himself. When you see Jesus, you'll either push Him away or push your sinfulness away. Instead of letting Peter run from what he felt, Jesus challenged him to a total reset.

Jesus consoled Simon, "Do not fear." Then, He roped him into something more scary than his sinking boat: "From now on you will be taking men alive."

Pete's trade changed. His "90 day trial" was up. Jesus graduated him to apprentice in this new discipline. Rock on!

Of course, He did not leave out Andrew who first brought Peter to "come and see." To them both, Jesus said, "Come after

---

282 Luke 5:8, LITV.

Me, and I will make you fishers of men."[283] They dropped their nets and followed Him that very moment.[284] They were leaving behind their identity and their income.

The other fishermen were also shaken over what had just happened.[285] James and John, sons of long-time fisherman Zebedee and business partners with Simon, took special note of what they had just experienced.[286] They would never see Jesus the same again either.

When the ships had made it to harbor, James and John had sat down in their dad's boat and started putting in new rope where the nets had ripped.[287] Jesus invited them to be fishermen in the new Kingdom. They dropped what they were doing and resigned from their roles in their dad's business.[288]

In the culture of that day, an honorable son carried on his father's trade. For them to leave their dad behind like that showed how huge their loyalty to Jesus had become. To them, Jesus was their new Father.

That catch of fish would have made them a lot of money. But they walked off from it.[289] Immediately. Those months with Him in Cana, Jerusalem, and Samaria had left their mark. They wanted more to life than what they had known. They were ready to leave it all and be trained by Him.

The call this time is not just to come and see Jesus but to "follow Me." Our fascination with Him leads to a new life purpose: to become what He is. They were to follow the King and

---

[283] Matthew 4:19, LITV. See also Mark 1:17.

[284] See Matthew 4:20 and Mark 1:18.

[285] See Luke 5:9.

[286] See Luke 5:10.

[287] See Mark 1:19 and Matthew 4:21.

[288] See Matthew 4:22 and Mark 1:20.

[289] See Luke 5:11.

learn life in His Kingdom. It was a commitment to transformation, not mere observation.

Jesus did not move too quickly when getting to this point. I have scared people off by rushing this before. I see potential in them and then start talking about what ministry they will do for the Lord before they have even come to know Him. We must not get ahead of a person's motivation.

These disciples show us how we should respond to Jesus: "forsaking all things, they followed Him."[290] Have you heard that call yet? Will you drop everything and everyone important to you?

Will you be trained by Jesus into doing His trade skill? Will your life be about catching an income and mending nets? Or will it be about catching people alive and mending broken hearts?

"Forsaking all" meant they left behind financial security, friends, family, and business partnerships. They made themselves totally dependent on Jesus. Now, you can see how Jesus does not offer a simple upgrade.

This isn't Humanity 2.0. Jesus's factory reset gives us the proper operating system our defective births did not include. We must be born from above to operate on His level.

Think of what these fishermen understood from what Jesus said. I think of fishing as a fun thing to do on a lazy weekend. To them, catching fish was exhausting work. We think of fishing as a solitary sport with a rod and reel; they knew it as a team pulling a net to shore.

Jesus called them to a team occupation, not a hobby. Fishermen worked in pairs. They would put the same effort and focus into hauling people into the Kingdom. Jesus had illustrated

---

290 Luke 5:11, LITV.

what it would look like if they did it His way: so many would come rushing in that nothing manmade could hold them.

RELIGIOUS DEMONS

A PPARENTLY THE MIRACULOUS CATCH of fish happened on a Friday morning because "immediately" it was Sabbath. Jesus led His followers to the Capernaum synagogue.[291] He was teaching them by His actions.

The King of the universe had invited a few to train as His assistants—like a US President selecting his cabinet members. More than just follow and watch, they were learning what to do from Him. The incognito King stepped up and taught in the Jewish meeting house.

The custom then was to hear from a visiting man (in good standing). The attendees did not know Jesus's true identity, but they sensed that something was very different. He was not speaking like a scholar or a rabbi like they had heard before. Most educated speakers simply quoted other great thinkers, borrowing others' thoughts and repeating them. That was their celebrated form of teaching.

---

[291] The book of Luke tells this story before the catch of fish; Mark tells it afterward. Mark 1:21 uses language that indicates he has the chronological sequence here. Luke 4:31 indicates that the stories regarding Capernaum come with no specific order.

Churches seem to snuggle into scholarly authority. They like educated and degreed speakers. Jesus talked with a different kind of authority that moved people, not a power to impress but a power to transform.

The Lord was not quoting Dr. ShrinkWrap to prove His case. He had more than book knowledge. He had no Master's degree, but He is the Master. He had no Doctorate, but when it comes to your spiritual condition, He can doctor it!

Jesus did not need a script. He is the Word. The religious scholars in Jerusalem had been shocked by His mastery of the message when He was just a youth.[292]

Like the people in Nazareth, the residents of Capernaum were also shocked as they heard the words of wisdom and life flowing from His mouth.[293] Unlike Nazareth, they did not run Him out of the synagogue. Yet.

However, Jesus did face a conflict. A demonized man spoke up.[294] The demon appears to have been defending the *status quo* in the synagogue: "Leave us alone!"[295]

That evil spirit—the first recorded demon Jesus dealt with—showed up at "church"! An evil spirit had found safe refuge in the religious center. Why? Because the Holy Spirit was not there.

Are there evil spirits in your church? You might never know if Jesus does not show up. Religious systems are great hiding places for bad spirits of pride, selfishness, guilt, greed, sexual sin, and condemnation.

---

[292] See Luke 2:48.

[293] See Mark 1:22 and Luke 4:32.

[294] See Mark 1:23, Luke 4:33.

[295] See Mark 1:24, Luke 4:34.

So many religious institutions have not only housed evil but spread it. Some church groups teach doctrines of demons.[296] We cannot think that religious behavior and religious structures make us safe—even if the name "Christian" is over the building.

Apparently a man who faithfully attended synagogue was demon-controlled. He was among people full of Bible knowledge yet evil reigned within him. Some demon-controlled people lead certain "Bible" focused groups today.

The people with scholarly mentions did not recognize Jesus for who He was, but the devil saw Him immediately. "What have we to do with You, Jesus of Nazareth?"[297] By mentioning Nazareth, was the evil spirit mocking Jesus about His recent painful rejection in His home town?

Knowing that he only had eternal punishment to look forward to, the spirit asked, "Have You come to destroy us?"[298] Demons see Jesus clearly but it does them no good. The role of evil spirits is to keep humans from seeing Jesus, lest they repent. Living humans still can turn from their sin; demons cannot.

That demon had insight that the spiritually blind congregation did not have: "I know You, who You are, the Holy One of God."[299] Unlike the Bible believers, the evil one saw that Jesus was the Holy One.[300] Demons already believe in the one God and they shudder at the thought of Him.[301] Perhaps that was why the man went into a seizure.

Jesus did not allow the spirit to dominate the moment or spill secrets about Him. "Be quiet!" or perhaps more literally, "Be

---

296 See I Timothy 4:1.

297 Mark 1:24, NKJV.

298 Mark 1:24, LITV.

299 Luke 4:34, LITV.

300 As stated in Psalm 16:10; 89:18-19.

301 See James 2:19.

muzzled!" He told it. Then He commanded it, "Come out of him!"[302]

Boom.

The evil spirit convulsed the man, threw him down in front of everyone, and then came out of him.[303] Though it made a lot of noise,[304] it "did not hurt him."[305]

Often demons will speak or manifest in some way in a person when they know they are about to get evicted. It is an attempt to dominate through fear. Some people become afraid when they see this. It was the spirit's last-ditch effort to regain control.

I imagine that demon went running to his other demon friends and told them, "Get your body and get out of town, I already lost mine!" If Jesus is your King, you can also throw these imposters out. We will learn more from Him about that later.

Jesus had power to teach and power to deliver. His trainees stood by and watched all this. Perhaps they did not realize they, too, would soon be operating under the power of the King and doing exactly these things: giving powerful instruction to humans and commanding the demons to leave.

Humans need to be reset. Demons must be removed. Don't confuse the two.

The religiously polished people responded to what they saw: "What word is this, that He commands the unclean spirits with authority and power, and they come out?"[306] They were

---

[302] Mark 1:25, LITV.
[303] See Luke 4:35.
[304] See Mark 1:26.
[305] Luke 4:35, NKJV.
[306] Luke 4:36, LITV. See also Mark 1:27.

trying to process that moment through their experience. Who had ever controlled a demon with words?

Where did His authority come from? Where did He get this new teaching? They had never heard it before. People were talking about Him in "every place of the neighborhood."[307]

The real amazing thing here is that that these Bible experts were amazed. Jesus had not come with something new. He came as Scripture in the flesh! He was living out every word of the Bible they so carefully guarded, rolled up in scrolls, and carefully stowed through the week.

The religious people had become experts on what people were saying about the Bible. Were they becoming followers of thinkers from past and present instead of experts on every word proceeding from the mouth of God? Perhaps Jesus's power and His person seemed so unusual and "new" because they had tired of the established and faithful Writings.

Today, the Christian scene is cluttered with bestselling books full of tips, tricks, and methods not from Scripture but popular culture. When you talk about things that are biblical, people think you are inventing something new. Who does church the way the apostles did? Who makes disciples the way Jesus did? Do we have His power or just stories about it?

---

[307] Luke 4:37, LITV.

COMMAND DISEASE

J ESUS DID NOT NEED the fame. He was looking for followers, apprentices, disciples. News about Him spread rapidly across Galilee—everyone was talking about it.[308] Soon, people in Nazareth would be saying, "I wish He would come here and do some miracles like He has in Capernaum," just as Jesus predicted.

Is Jesus all about the fame for you? Or are you a follower? Are you learning from Him and then doing what He does? Or are you just waving a pennant and shouting rah-rahs for Jesus?

Every religious system will eventually become merely a human institution. God's appointed Temple did.[309] You can see this with many Christian denominations over time. Next, they can become demon strongholds.

The Pharisees began as a lively movement of returning to the ways of God. Many synagogues throughout Galilee were

---

[308] See Mark 1:28.

[309] See Jeremiah 2:27; 32:33; 44:17; Ezekiel 8:16-18; Joel 1:13-15; 2:15-18; Acts 7:42-43.

influenced by these revivalists. Now demons coexisted among them, while they studied Scripture and fellowshipped together.

Jesus spoke and outed the demon at church. Is your religion full of authority and power? Or is it a safe haven for demons? Do you speak and serve the Lord with power and authority? Or is it routine and predictable?

After leaving church (the synagogue), Rocky invited Jesus over to his house for a barbeque (with chicken and beef of course, not pork).[310] Peter and his brother Andrew shared this home, but old Pete's wife had brought her mother to live there, too. They invited their former business partners James and John and the other disciples over for the meal.[311]

When they entered the house, Simon discovered that mom-in-law was not doing well at all. She had a deadly fever.[312] They told Jesus at once about this situation.

The King has compassion on those in need. He stood over the suffering woman and spoke to the fever the way He spoke to demons. He "rebuked" it.[313] Speaking to it sharply in no uncertain terms, Jesus showed that He holds authority over disease.

Taking Peter's mother-in-law by the hand, Jesus raised her up. Instantly, her fever left her and she helped them all get something to eat. Jesus did these things because He loved people.

He would never beg an evil spirit to come out of someone; He simply commanded them. We never read of Him bargaining

---

[310] The law of Moses forbid the eating of an animal that did not chew it's cud, which made pigs taboo. We don't know what they did eat at this particular meal.

[311] See Mark 1:29.

[312] See Mark 1:30 and Luke 4:38.

[313] Mark 1:31, LITV.

with disease or praying for it to go away. He simply spoke and it was done.

Think of what the disciples have seen firsthand to this point. With no natural explanation, fish overloaded the net—demonstrating how people will come into the Kingdom. The demon was evicted before all in the synagogue—showing that the religious program had no power and needed Jesus. Now, a close relative and friend has been healed of a fast-moving disease—revealing that Jesus can reverse the effects of sin in one's life.

Thinking back now to what they saw at the Temple. Jesus's mission includes uprooting religious ruts. Money-making and bureaucracy had overrun the Temple. Many churches today are about manmade programs, routines, and money. While most churches are not profitable enterprises, if a local congregation determines everything on the basis of budgets, the measurement tool is all wrong.

The Temple was to be a place to teach people about the Lord. He could hardly be seen when He came to visit though, because they had made religion about everything else but Him. The local synagogues had, too. Nazareth ran Him off, and the demonized church attender challenged Him in Capernaum.

Jesus is not a church-house phenomenon. He works in homes, on lakes, at weddings, and on the road. His followers are learning the adaptability and "everywhere" nature of the Kingdom.

Christianity is not just good moral teaching about better behavior. Many books/programs help one be a better person. In Jesus, we have the power to overcome, to live from above.

The disciples are learning. They have gone from being unconsciously unaware of the Kingdom to now being consciously unaware. They traveled with Jesus for a few months and slowly had their eyes opened to how massive this Kingdom was. They learned that they had no idea what the Kingdom was like. It was not going to be some little fortress in Jerusalem; it would not be limited to the borders of Israel.

There are four stages of Kingdom living. We all start out unaware of the Kingdom of God. The first phase is called "unconsciously unaware" or in other words, we don't know we don't know.

When someone shares the message of the Kingdom with us, we realize we don't know what we need to know about the King's domain. Thus, we are now consciously unaware; we recognize that we need to learn about this new thing. Jesus's recruits were at this stage now. They would be for a while.

As they grew, they became consciously aware of the Kingdom. They later learned to share the message with others and invite them to know the King and live in His domain. But wait, there's more!

When Jesus's mission was complete, the disciples would be so fully immersed in the Kingdom they would not think about it. Then, they would be unconsciously aware. Representing the King and living by His power will be their new default, the factory reset being complete. If you haven't reached this point, your persistence in following the King will lead you to the place where you think His thoughts, live His desires, and sense His presence in all you do.

Their eyes were still opening. At this point, Jesus's trainees were definitely onto step two on the stairway of their spiritual changeover:

IV. Unconsciously aware

III. Consciously aware

II. Consciously unaware

I. Unconsciously unaware

After a year with the Master, they will reach the 3rd step.[314] They will go into action, putting the Kingdom first in all they say and do. They will expand it everywhere, making more disciples themselves.

After the Spirit comes, the apostles will be so deeply immersed in the Kingdom they will not even think about it. Disciple-making will flow naturally from them at that fourth point of progress. Like a fish in water does not know it is wet, a fully formed disciple is saturated with Kingdom and only sees life through that lens.

Which step are you on?

Although being a disciple of Jesus is like a student/professor relationship, this is not a community college. No one comes to Jesus and volunteers. The Lord picks His own team.

You are here because He is drawing you. You are being recruited. It is a privilege to be called.

Those business owners and workers were willing to leave their careers behind to follow the Rabbi. They wanted to be trained by the King. Do you?

Who wouldn't want to spend time with the King of their country? Who wouldn't want to be trained to expand His Kingdom? He will provide everything you need.

---

[314] For visual details on this topic, see page 42 of the *Handbook for your Factory Reset*.

TOUCH OF DELIVERANCE

A YOUNG MAN WANTED TO LEARN to work with jade. This valuable, green stone fascinated the youth and he felt he wanted to spend his life tooling and selling it. He applied to a jade expert and the master agreed to apprentice him. "Come tomorrow and I will begin instructing you."

The next day, the young man showed up promptly. His instructor put a jade stone in his hand, saying, "Hold onto this." The young man looked the stone over, turning it, feeling it, and examining it. Each morning when he came to the workshop, the skilled instructor would put a piece of jade in his hand and then go to work, saying nothing more to him the rest of the day.

After days of simply holding a jade stone, the youth grew discouraged. Finally, at the end of a day of doing nothing but holding the stone he spoke up, "I hoped for more than this. I thought you were going to apprentice me to work with jade."

"Fair enough," the master said. "Come back tomorrow and we shall begin."

Feeling a little more hopeful, the young apprentice arrived at the shop early the next morning. The expert had him sit in his same chair. Then, without a word, the master handed the young man a rock and said, "Hold this."

"That's not jade!" the youth cried out.

"Excellent," said the master, "you have just passed the first lesson."[315]

Spending time with Jesus is not just about learning who He is. It is also about learning who He is not. That is why we are taking a slow pace as we learn of Him.

You've read over 50 chapters already (counting *Seeing Jesus*), and we only have a few glimpses to what He is about. We only have a few hints of what the Kingdom is. No clear definitions. No academic dissertations. Just a few stories to go on.

The stories do go on. For days and weeks and months the disciples traveled with the Master and learned what the Kingdom of God was not. They held Jesus close and learned to identify the counterfeit because they knew the Real so well.

You must pass this first lesson. There are many counterfeit-jesus systems. Do not grow weary in this process of learning to identify the Truth.

Jesus got in trouble with the establishment in Capernaum because one was not to tend the medical needs of people on the Sabbath (except for life-threatening situations). One could not travel more than half a mile on Saturdays either. When Jesus healed Simon's mother-in-law on a Sabbath, He was "flying under the radar" because she was at home and none of the legalists could see what happened to condemn Him for it.

As the sun descended on that day of mandatory rest, people were again able to walk as far as they pleased. They came

---

[315] Hull, *Jesus Christ Disciple Maker*, 33-34.

from everywhere to find Jesus.[316] The "whole city was gathered at the door."[317]

The synagogue could have been a healing place, but it wasn't. In that place sat the Writings about the Healer. Yet the establishment did not permit the "work" of the Anointed on His day.

A church building is only useful to the level that Jesus is at work there. The churches after the time of Jesus sprang up in homes, not specially designated buildings. God does not wait to perform healings at shrines or chapels. The street will do.

Jesus is the House of God. Wherever He showed up, there God was. Like He told the woman at the well: worship is not a location but in Spirit and Truth.

The story got out about Jesus lifting Simon's mother-in-law from her death bed. Then, everyone, "as many as had sick ones with various diseases, brought them to Him."[318] Jesus personally touched each one, healing them.

That personal contact posed a problem on two levels. First, a man was not to touch a woman, let alone talk to her. Jesus wouldn't let their legalism keep Him from transforming someone's life. Second, according to the law of Moses, a person was not to touch a diseased person or they would become unclean themselves. The "clean" of Jesus was stronger than the unclean of this polluted world.

This story illustrates how the Kingdom is not bound by manmade walls. The Kingdom is wherever the King's presence is. Jesus makes whole whatever has been torn and broken, if we bring it to Him.

---

[316] See Luke 4:40.
[317] Mark 1:33, LITV.
[318] Luke 4:40, LITV.

Centuries before, Isaiah had told about the One who would restore what had been broken:

> "Surely He has borne our griefs
> And carried our sorrows."[319]

From this passage, we get hope because our Lord will heal wounded emotions. Grief can paralyze and sorrow can deform. The Anointed One takes both on Himself, healing the broken-hearted.

But that is not all.

The Gospel of Matthew brings new insights to that quote. Saying Jesus healed all who were sick, it offers this translation:

> "He Himself took our infirmities
> And bore our sicknesses."[320]

The verse suddenly extends to not only hidden wounds but to physical ones as well. What kind of sickness and disease does Jesus heal? All!

Many believers expect Jesus to take away all sorrow. We turn to the Lord to heal our grief. Yet, a prevailing mindset still tells even the most faithful Christians that healing is random and you never can be sure the Lord will do it for you. Our faith for recovery from grief and sorrow comes from the same verse that gives us hope for restoration of physical pains and deficiencies, too. We trust our King for healing because His Kingdom can manipulate matter, reminding us "nothing is impossible."[321]

Disease is a physical illustration of what sin does to a person. In this Kingdom of Life there is no decay. The ravages of sin are reversed by the Healer. Miracle healings show us visually what happens spiritually to our inner person.

---

319 Isaiah 53:4, NKJV.
320 Matthew 8:17, NKJV.
321 See Luke 1:37.

Another dramatic evidence of the Kingdom involves another kingdom. The kingdom of darkness includes evil spirits that oppress, depress, and stress available people. Our King and His Kingdom drive those out as well.

Having heard about the demon eviction at the synagogue earlier that day, people brought their demonized friends to Jesus. Jesus dealt with demons differently than He did with the people who were sick. Where He did not cringe at touching bodies victimized by decay, it appears He never touched those inhabited by a demon. Instead, He spoke, casting them out "with a word."[322]

Demons would speak out when they got near Jesus. They would share information about Him: "You are the Anointed [King], the Son of God!"[323] They knew He was the chosen King and they knew about His Kingdom. Jesus did not allow them to speak. Evil spirits knew some facts about Jesus.[324] The demon in the synagogue had called Him the "Holy One."

Jesus did not allow such outbursts: "he cast out many demons, and He did not allow the demons to speak, because they knew Him."[325] Though demons can speak spiritual truths, they do not have divine illumination. They have to accept the realities in the unseen realm, but they do not love these truths.

Many Christians think salvation comes by believing information about Jesus as the Savior, that He died on the cross, etc. Thus, for them, reaching others is all about information transfer. Demons accept that knowledge and shake in fear about this One God.[326] Yet that does not save them. The evil kingdom

---

[322] Matthew 8:16, NKJV.

[323] See Luke 4:41, most translations have "Anointed" as "Christ."

[324] Part of the mystery of Christ they did not know. If they had, the ruling spirits would not have worked to destroy Him. I Corinthians 2:7-8.

[325] Mark 1:34, LITV.

[326] See James 2:13.

does not submit to the Lordship of Jesus. Those who abandon their own interests to this Man are the ones rescued in Him.

Jesus did not engage devils in a conversation. How about you? Do you forbid the enemy to speak in your life?

Jesus had invited the disciples to follow and learn from Him how to "net" people. Part of hauling people into the Kingdom involves delivering them from demons and healing their bodies. Neither can be done by human power, only as agents of Jesus's power. He is the King. The King commissions servants and messengers to do His works.

In my early attempts at reaching people for Jesus, a friend and I met at a couple's house to talk about the Bible. As we went to leave, we all prayed together. The presence of Jesus showed up as we prayed.

Looking over at the young husband, I noticed he was shaking heavily. I reached out to him and suddenly he dropped to the floor screaming. The demon in him was terrified of the presence of Jesus. The man's mouth opened larger than humanly possible and his face contorted as the groans of anguish escaped his soul.

"In the name of Jesus, come out of him!" we said. In a moment, the spirit departed and the man was in his right mind. He told us afterward that it was a spirit of pain—all the hurts and sorrows he had carried left him.

Casting out demons is not a recreational enterprise. There are some people who chase the paranormal to make sensational videos or satisfy personal curiosity. There are some who evict demons for hire, though it is debatable how effective their cures are.

In the first century, there were Jewish exorcists. Seven brothers tried casting out a demon using the name of Jesus, but the demon knew they did not belong to Jesus and so he ripped up their clothes and wounded them.[327] Demons are not afraid of mere humans, but they know the King has more power than what is in their whole kingdom combined.

Later in the Christian story, a missionary named Paul had a slave girl following his team shouting that they were servants of the most-high God. This was factually true, but it was a bitter knowledge, not a joyful revelation. Finally, Paul cast the demon out of this woman. She could no longer answer the 1-900-number psychic hotline or read palms for her owners.[328]

Spiritual insights should flow from above, not beneath. We need to hear from God who He is. Revelation should flow out of relationship. People access inside info by being close to Him.

The devils knew if they could expose who Jesus was, the human enemies would turn on Him faster. The devil plays dirty. You cannot out-bargain him.

---

[327] See Acts 19:14.

[328] See this story for yourself at Acts 16:16-19.

ONWARD MISSION

THE SUN HUNG ON THE EDGE of the ridge for a while and looked settled enough to stay. Then, in the last throws of its journey for the day, its red beams fingered through the clouds. It slowly painted the hills and lakeshore with a orangish hue which grew weaker by the minute. As soon as the last sliver of sunlight slipped behind the western horizon, people began to scurry.

Actually, some had already started walking before the sun dropped. They would get in the last few paces they had left of their allotted half mile for that Sabbath day. Once the sun disappeared the new day started, and they could walk as far as they pleased.

Following the example set in Genesis, Jews started each new day at sundown. Saturday had ending; it was now Sunday (which Christians later called "the Lord's Day"). Where were the residents of Capernaum heading in the fading afterglow of daylight? To see Jesus.

Moses had first written the ordinances regarding Sabbath observance. However, he did not have the power to restore the broken and hurting. Our Lord (risen on a new day) can turn any evil around.

No doubt Jesus was busy late into the night when the whole town of Capernaum came to Simon and Andrew's house to seek healing and deliverance from demons. He did not sleep long, though. Soon, "rising up quite early in the night, He went out and went away into a deserted place."[329]

In the stories of Abraham, David, and other heroes of the faith, we see many positive things said about early morning prayer. One of my family's heroes, Nona Freeman, was not a morning person but she had many powerful prayer times at 2 AM. There is something special about getting alone with the Lord in the single-digit hours of the morning.

Jesus did not just get up early, like 6 or 7. It literally said He got up while it was still night. There was no rule or requirement that He do this, but there was something He knew about getting up while it was still dark.

For one thing, since people are not up and active there are fewer distractions at that time of day. Also, the spirit world is not as active either and early-morning prayer becomes prime time to set the spiritual events of the day in order. Perhaps you also will discover the Lord in a new way during those early hours.

I've often wondered what Jesus's prayers were like. Crowded by needy people, this Man knew He had to stay on mission. Even when physically exhausted, He prioritized prayer. He prayed because that is what the original factory design for humans is—our operating system requires this daily scan, debug, and updates.

Jesus did not force the disciples to pray with Him. He didn't even invite them. He did not pray at the house or in the courtyard where others could hear Him. He did not pray loud so

---

[329] Mark 1:35, LITV.

His trainees would feel guilty and pray as well. He left them behind.

He found a deserted place, a lonely place.[330] His disciples were not praying with Him. They were not praying at all. What was He praying for? Who was He praying for?

As the sun came up that Sunday morning, more people showed up at the house. They were looking for Jesus because they, too, wanted to be healed. Simon probably felt overwhelmed (and under-rested). He ran around looking for Jesus. When Jesus had said "Follow Me" did He mean for them to follow Him in prayer too?

Those people came with real needs—real people needed real help. Where was the miracle Man? It is not a surprise that Jesus was hard to find. His own parents lost Him at age twelve. Now His followers cannot locate Him.

Finally, Rocky and some others found Jesus.[331] His parents had found Him discussing the Scriptures; His disciples found Him praying. If you are alone and away from everyone else, what could you be found doing?

A human must like to hear the words, "Everyone is looking for you."[332] It's nice to have people grab ahold of you and beg you to stay. Some of the locals held Jesus tightly so He would not get away from them.[333] If He came to feel validated and accepted, their kindness would have kept Him. If Jesus had come to heal disease, this would have been a rewarding moment.

He had not come for those reasons. He came to awaken people to the presence of a new Kingdom. Healing and deliverance were only part of that.

---

[330] See Luke 4:42.
[331] See Mark 1:36.
[332] See Mark 1:37.
[333] See Luke 4:42.

Jesus seems to have ignored their plea. "Let's go," He said. "It is right for Me to proclaim the gospel, the kingdom of God, to the other cities, because I was sent on this mission."[334]

This is one of those times you don't want to ask, "What would Jesus do?" You probably shouldn't ask that if you see a Temple full of money-changers either. As He leaves the town where people had come to love Him so much, we scratch our heads. Why would He just walk off and leave them like that?

Many in ministry today wear themselves out trying to fill every request, please every person. What began as serving God became a matter of serving needs. Is it time to reset your thinking and actions? Busyness is not next to godliness.

The stereotypical pastor answers every phone call, runs to every "emergency," and babysits every issue that arises. Such a person often comes to the brink of total collapse from this "Messiah complex." Even the Messiah did not have such a hero complex of thinking He had to do everything everyone asked of Him.

The exhausted leader feels even more pain when those same people turn against him or her. Jesus knew that many of the ones He was helping would one day turn against Him. He was not doing ministry to build His own self-worth.

Jesus was not destroyed by "compassion fatigue." Many religious people today give care to others until they destroy their own selves. Of course Jesus was moved by compassion, but He was not ruled by it. He knew He would one day be wounded in the house of His friends.[335]

He was ruled by the larger goal: making people aware of the Kingdom. Miracles simply showed what the Kingdom was

---

334 Luke 4:43, LITV and see Mark 1:38.
335 See Zechariah 13:6.

like. He did not come to heal everyone in Israel. Some have mistaken miracles as evidence of the Lord's favor.

Miracles are not His ultimate goal. They are a big deal to us, but easy for Him. A big deal to Him is a human who totally abandons his or her own desires for the Lord and His Kingdom work.

The community still had diseased people needing a cure and demons needing eviction. Jesus was like, "We're out of here." The modern pastor would say, "Oh lookie, a crowd!" Jesus said, "Gotta go!"

Popularity had become a problem. People were so focused on solving immediate needs that He could not preach to their real need. They wanted the miracle, not the message.

If God called you to a purpose, don't waste time doing something else. The disciples learned from Jesus's example. They appointed workers so they could return their focus to prayer and the ministry of the Word.[336]

Author Steven Covey pointed out that many people exhaust themselves on the "urgent" things of life. Is that how you will follow Jesus? Urgent things include: a ringing phone, a whining dog, a knock at the door.

Sometimes churches build ministries that create more urgent crises: daycare, soup kitchen, bake sale. Can you house every homeless person? Can you feed every hungry person? Can you do every fundraiser, outreach program, and other good idea?

Rather than running after the urgent stuff, shouldn't we follow Jesus's mission? Aren't we here to get people to see the Kingdom and call them to the devoted life? What would change if that was your focus?

---

[336] See Acts 6:2-3.

Too many people come to the Lord by addition rather than submission. This crowd had come by attraction rather than subtraction. They wanted to add Jesus into their portfolio but not take anything out.

Disciples are those who have beached their boats. If they won't submit to the Lord, He will not commit to them. Miracles might come but they won't obey Him. He will not be in them. The Kingdom brings life change at the core of a person.

If the leader prayed a great while before life started for the day, how could the followers benefit from this? What did He do in prayer that made it meaningful and not feel alone though no one was with Him? What was He praying about? Who was He praying for?

As you learn more about serving the Lord, you will find yourself drained by this life of service. It takes a strength from outside you to restore your energy. Our strength comes from His joy.[337]

Prayer for many people can become a drudgery. Jesus appears to have found it a time to recharge. We will learn more from Him on this later.

---

[337] See Psalm 21:1 and Nehemiah 8:10.

JESUS HEALS

PEOPLE HAD CROWDED all around Jesus. It would be nearly impossible for Him to walk out of Capernaum without them following Him. The lake would be His quickest escape. Peter's boat didn't stay beached for long.[338] Jesus not only preached from his boat, but ol' Rocky got to chauffer Him to many locations.

Jesus and His disciples jumped onboard to head to other cities. Perhaps this is why He chose shore-side Capernaum as His base of operations for Galilee. From there, He could reach the various coast cities of Galilee, Decapolis (to the east), and Perea (southeast) if necessary.

Jesus did three things as He traveled in Galilee: He taught, proclaimed, and healed.[339] He still does those things today through His disciples. Anything opposed to any one of these Kingdom functions is counterfeit. We will talk about each one in turn.

---

[338] See Matthew 8:18 and Matthew 9:1.

[339] See Matthew 4:23.

Teaching. In the synagogues, He found people who knew and loved the Scriptures. There, He could open the Scrolls as He did in Nazareth and explain the message that was written. That was teaching.

Not everyone is ready to be taught. To learn, one must first admit they don't know something. Teaching requires an agreed-upon basis from which the teacher builds the student's understanding. This is why teaching will work well with people who love the Scriptures. You, for example, are reading this book because you have a foundational love for God's Word and are willing to grow.

Proclaiming. Jesus did the proclaiming, or "preaching" as we often call it, everywhere—in homes, in streets, from a docked boat, and in the synagogues.[340] He announced the nearness of the Kingdom and created greater awareness. Apparently you could not separate His preaching and the result of demons coming out.[341]

A "herald" would walk the streets of a kingdom and proclaim news from the king to the citizens. Jesus was the King walking the streets of Israel proclaiming His new Kingdom. His followers later would announce Him and see the same dramatic results of healing and demons cast out.[342]

Healing. Healings give a visual, tangible expression of the Kingdom. Proclaiming brings awareness that God is doing something. Teaching gives details about what God is doing to those who are already interested. Healing illustrates what the Kingdom is like. Kingdom proclamation and instruction come with Kingdom demonstration.

---

[340] See Luke 4:44.
[341] See Mark 1:39.
[342] See Matthew 10:25 and Luke 6:40.

Wherever Jesus traveled, He was "healing every disease and every sickness among the people."[343] These were not just runny noses or imaginary pains. The crowds "brought to Him all sick people who were afflicted with various diseases and torments, and those who were demon-possessed, epileptics, and paralytics; and He healed them."[344]

When people heard about the miracles, they crowded to see Jesus. He did not even have to leave Galilee. People came from thirty miles away and more. Not only did the reports about Him bring people from the south in Jerusalem and Judea, but also the area of Perea to the east of the Jordan River. People came from east of Galilee, too, out of the confederacy of Decapolis—a mostly Gentile area.[345]

To the north, people in Gentile Syria also came down.[346] Many Jews left their cities to come see Jesus. Since Decapolis, Syria, and even much of Galilee had so many Gentiles, it would not be surprising to know that many of those healed and converted were non-Jews.

Unfortunately, many of these became interested only in the healings and not in changing their ways or pursuing the Kingdom. Thus, they could suppress the message Jesus came to give. Similar things happen today when a group gets too focused on miracles and healings instead of the King and the message of His Kingdom.

A young man went to a meeting where the power of the Kingdom was at work. The one proclaiming Jesus walked into the crowd and saw the young man's leg in a cast. He had come because his family brought him, not but because of a hunger for the Lord.

---

343 Matthew 4:23, LITV.
344 Matthew 4:24, NKJV.
345 See Matthew 4:25.
346 See Matthew 4:24.

The preacher looked at him and said, "God will heal your leg." When the preacher saw the can of chewing tobacco tucked in the top of his leg cast, he said, "He'll take your tobacco addiction away, too!"

The young man snatched up the can before the preacher could and said, "No He won't."

God healed the man's leg anyway. He walked out on a perfectly healed bone and they were able to remove the cast. He did not choose to walk with the King.

Some Christian movements have become all about healings and miracles. They end up being experiential, chasing after demonstrations of the Spirit but lack the teaching of the Kingdom. This is as counterfeit as ghost busters. No wonder many such institutions become demonic as they simply chase after supernatural things without discerning Kingdom fullness.

An opposite problem also exists. There are those who call themselves Christian who do not believe in the power of the Kingdom today. They promote teaching and preaching while rejecting healing, which includes casting out demons. They say healing is not for our time and that the miracle power of Jesus has ceased. While it is wrong to make the Kingdom all about chasing miracles, it is just as wrong to say such things have ceased.

The nearness of the Kingdom triggered miracles then. Why would miracles cease if the Kingdom is with us now? Perhaps those who see Jesus through the filter of "miracles have ceased" are looking at the wrong kingdom. Perhaps they are seeing a false jesus. Or maybe they never considered that they can have access to Kingdom power. We must know the real so we can spot the counterfeit.

Don't be shocked that Christian religions would be blind to Jesus. Remember that Jesus was casting demons out in synagogues—the assembly houses of the faithful believers. Many churches today also need demons removed because they, like those dead gatherings, have not discerned their purpose or the true Kingdom. Many churches have spiritual power that did not come from above.

Why would the devil show up at church? Because governments, businesses, schools, and other institutions are already in the world system and doomed. In the gatherings of worship the devil works harder because he must stop the Kingdom.

If the Kingdom of God advances, the kingdom of darkness has to shutter some doors. The devil does not want to go out of business. Demons have more to accomplish in a church business meeting than they do in a commercial business. Sometimes what looks like personality clashes could be spiritual manifestations.

Obviously, demonized people need Jesus to set them free from the power of the evil one. So do those with illness or physical deficiency. The devil impairs people both physically and spiritually. The Holy Spirit worked powerfully in Jesus of Nazareth to travel around, "healing all those having been oppressed by the devil."[347] When the Lord miraculously cures someone, we see measureable, tangible evidence that the enemy's power has been broken.

What did Jesus do because He was swarmed by people needing help? He got away alone and prayed. Often, "He was drawing back in a deserted place, and praying."[348] This would be key for His followers as well, but they had not learned it yet.

How do you keep up with the overwhelm of giving care? Pray. Want evidence of the Kingdom in your life? Pray. Get away and talk to the Lord!

---

[347] Acts 10:38, LITV. Of course, this is not to say that every disease is a demonic manifestation.

[348] Luke 5:16, LITV.

For me, my "deserted place" is early in the morning. After the sun is up, family, friends, ministry obligations, and so much more demand my focus. I have to talk to Him alone and at this phase in my life, alone is a time of day rather than a location where no one can find me. You have to find your spiritual getaway, too.

Jesus did not get bogged down trying to solve every issue or change every mind, neither should His followers. Some people are blinded by religious filters. Move on! Get over the Messiah complex of trying to be the answer for every problem.

Know your place and walk in that—not a million good possibilities. Do what you were made to be great at. If you are just looking to ride a wave of popularity, you will be burned. Whatever you do, do it with Kingdom power.

The Pharisees saw Jesus's crowds and got jealous. They did not care about the results or that people were being helped. They wanted things done according to their system. They wanted His crowd. The volatility of Jesus's work shook them up. Their religion was all about what humans could do, not the mighty power of God. They said prayers but had no results to show for it.

Jesus was not coming to offer Judaism 2.0. He had to introduce a Kingdom; so do we. His dramatic and powerful work showed that He had a bigger thing going than just recycling existing institutions. Just as bodies were made new, so would the inner person be, if they would let Jesus touch them.

Jesus works with each person on an individual basis. When He called Peter, the man had to leave his boat. Legalists would say that this means fishing is a sin. But Jesus did not condemn all fishermen. Simply put, Simon, Andrew, James, and John could not enter the Kingdom with a fishing net in their hands. Jesus's followers are growing and His purpose in their lives will be specific, as you will soon see when they return to Capernaum again.

MIRACLE OVER MESSAGE?

A MAN'S SKIN DISEASE had covered his body, making it "full of leprosy."[349] This could indicate a wide variety of chronic sores or other progressive skin diseases. Such a condition prevented a person from worshipping at the Temple. Those who were so diseased also had to live outside the city and call out "unclean" when they came around other people.

Those kind of symptoms also denied lepers access to the synagogue. Some Jewish meeting houses had a hole or holes in the wall where lepers could sit outside and peek through to hear the Scriptures being read. Life for them was more than dealing with physical discomfort but also the razor edge of social rejection.

What strengthened the social exclusion was the popular belief that all disease came from some sin or another. The prevailing assumption regarding skin diseases was that they had come on the person because they had slandered someone else. Since Miriam became leprous after speaking against her brother

---

[349] Luke 5:12, LITV.

Moses, someone popularized the idea that anyone with such a disease had also spoken badly against another.

Imagine the guilt, shame, and rejection this man must have faced. He is bold to come to Jesus after hearing great reports about His healing power. However, the first word out of his mouth shows he needed inner healing: "If."[350]

His conscious mind, has processed the facts and reasoned that there was a possibility that Jesus could cure him. However, at the core, he did not trust these thoughts. "Sure, Jesus can heal others, but me?" He worried that this all might be too good to be true.

He approached the Anointed One in self-humiliation: "falling on his face, he begged" for the Lord's mercy.[351] He thought Jesus might not help a guy like him. And why should He? The dude had been kicked around and pushed out his whole life.

But what would it hurt to try? You are going to fight those self-sabotaging thoughts in every step you take forward into the Kingdom. Your eyes see further than your reflex emotions can grasp.

He did not ask to be healed exactly, but to be cleansed. Biblically, a cured leper was referred to as "cleansed" not "healed." Skin diseases filled a different category than other illnesses.

Perhaps he was wanting more than just a restored body, but a cleansed social image. There had been a lot of junk-talk built up in his mind. Others had raked a lot of dirt and their comments had shaped his self-awareness.

---

[350] See Mark 1:41 and Matthew 8:2.
[351] Luke 5:12, LITV.

This is the healing you seek from the King, too. It's more than miracle changes in your body, but also how you see yourself. The question is not only if you can see Jesus, but can you see yourself the way Jesus sees you?

The diseased man needed the whole package deal (healing and cleansing) so he could deal with life again. He was asking for a total makeover, not just a better epidermis. You also, don't want to just look better, but to be new on the inside.

Today, the Lord heals the broken heart as easily as the broken bones. He restores the disgusting spirit as easily as gross skin issues. He transforms the emotions as easily as He breaks a fever.

That diseased man's "if" sounds like many Christians today. "Heal, if you will, Lord." Notice that Jesus healed every person who brought their problem to Him.[352] Jesus never turned someone away, saying, "Sorry don't want to." He never said, "I prefer that you continue to suffer like that, sorry."

Someone started the rumor that Jesus does not always want to heal us. Many church-goers say, "If God wills, He will heal." If that was true physically, it would be true spiritually. He wants to restore every broken heart.

Jesus said, "I will." He did not give a condition. If He's present, He will heal.

If it worked that way then, when did it change? Rather than believe and expect a miracle, many Christians have given themselves an easy out if nothing happens: "It must not have been God's will." Jesus says, "I will."

What are you asking of Jesus? "Lord, if you desire to make me whole—"

"I do desire that."

---

352 See Matthew 8:16.

"If you are willing to heal me—"

"I am willing."

If you thought Jesus was heartless when He left the needy crowd in Capernaum, think again. When He noticed the diseased man, it hit him in the gut. His insides literally moved with compassion.[353]

This was not just a business deal or a ritual—Jesus cared deeply about the man's condition. You better believe He is willing! Jesus reached out and touched the man.

Boom! Instantly the disease disappeared.[354] Jesus simply spoke the word.

The man couldn't remember the last time someone put a hand on his shoulder. Everyone else was afraid to. Just looking at him grossed them out. Perhaps you would understand how they felt if you imagine yourself touching a bleeding AIDS patient.

Jesus looked crazy to be touching the unclean man. Love took priority to Moses's orders about avoiding unclean people. The man no longer had to look down on himself, excuse himself from society, or warn others that he was a hazard.

Jesus does many cringe-worthy things to restore us. Did it hurt God's reputation to spend time on me with all my issues? He risked looking bad when He put His arm around me and made me whole. Nothing you have done is so embarrassing that Jesus would not reach out and restore you.

---

353 In Mark 1:41, the phrase "moved with compassion" comes from the literal Greek expression "His bowels churned" (*splagchnizomai*). A similar expression to day might be "it hit me in the pit of my stomach" or "it turned my stomach to see that." This phrase in the Greek, however, does not illustrate disgust but true empathy.

354 See Matthew 8:3; Mark 1:42; and Luke 5:13.

The cleansed man could now have a family. He could now hold a regular job. He could now go sit and hear the Scriptures next to the others who loved God.

This should have been enough to reset the man's loyalties. When your "if" to Jesus comes back as a "yes," let it transform you. His work is more than skin deep.

The King commanded his worshipping follower, "Go follow the protocol provided by Moses." This was a big order. The priest would have to verify that the man's skin was clear now. Then, he would put him in quarantine for a week to prove that the disease was not coming back.[355] That checkup would relieve other people's worries about the person still being contagious.

The details here paint a picture of the gospel. The law of Moses could not cleanse anyone, but it could declare if someone had been cleansed. Only Jesus could make that change; we find no previous biblical record of leprosy cleansed in Israel.

Jesus touched that man's disgusting body just like He has touched your sin. Just one touch took away your past and gave you hope for a new tomorrow. These signs reveal the Kingdom!

The King also "strictly" ordered the newly cleansed man that he should not tell anyone what had happened. In a very assertive way, Jesus told him not to tell others yet.[356] When issuing this order of silence, Jesus used the same kind of words He had used when He commanded demons to be quiet.[357]

Demons cannot choose to not obey Jesus. Humans have a choice. This human did not choose well.

---

[355] See Leviticus 14:1-32.

[356] See Matthew 8:4; Mark 1:43-44: and Luke 5:14.

[357] Greek *paraggello*, in Luke 5:14 to the man and to demons in Luke 8:29 and Acts 16:18. In Mark 1:44, the word is *embrimaomai*, meaning Jesus spoke to the man with very strong emotion—symbolized with the idea of snorting with anger (Thayer's). Jesus was very serious about this.

The Lord did not need hundreds of gawkers crowding Him because they would get in the way of His purpose. He had come to minister to more than just felt needs (disease) but to establish a Kingdom of committed people. Unfortunately, the man turned and began to tell everyone right away.

This healed man wanted Jesus's miracle but not His message. Many people today have those wrong values. They want Jesus to fix their problems, give them more money, and do amazing things. But after they bow before Him, do they rise to obey?

The loud-mouth leper began to tell everyone. Drama-seekers swamped Jesus like traffic going by a four-car pileup. Jesus would not minister in the cities after that.[358] "Plan B" took Him back to His favorite prayer location: the wilderness and deserted areas. Crowds came to Him from all over.[359]

There is a big difference between someone blessed by Jesus and a disciple of Him. A servant of the King follows His orders. What brought you to Jesus? What keeps you there? Do you take His orders or just seek His touch?

---

[358] See Mark 1:45.
[359] See Mark 1:45 and Luke 5:14.

TEARING IT UP!

JESUS AND COMPANY got back on the boat one day and returned "to His own city."[360] Last time He was in Capernaum,[361] He had worked late into the night healing many people. The next morning He took the crew out of town to tell other cities about the Kingdom. Now, He's back at home, His ministry headquarters (for the moment).

His house[362] became rather crowded as people flooded in from everywhere when they heard He was in town. "And the power of the Lord was there, for the curing of them."[363] Keeping the mission first, Jesus spoke the Word to a house so full of people that they were standing outside the house looking in.[364]

They came for their wants, but He also ministered to their needs. This time, religion pros (Pharisees and Bible teachers)

---

[360] Matthew 9:1, LITV.

[361] See Mark 2:1.

[362] After moving out of Nazareth, Jesus moved to Capernaum (see Matthew 4:13).

[363] Luke 5:17, LITV.

[364] See Mark 2:2.

had shown up.[365] In spite of those skeptics, the miracle power of the Lord was there to cure disease.

Four guys showed up carrying their friend.[366] They looked at the crowd and realized there was little chance for even one of them to get through that jam-packed group, let alone all five of them. These guys had probably carried their man all this way last time Jesus was in town only to miss Him when He slipped away. This time, they would not let Him get away.

Most homes in that area had flat roofs made of log beams, thatch, and almost two feet of mud. It served as a rooftop deck where the family could sleep on hot evenings rather than inside the stuffy building. To the side of the house, a staircase led to that skyline sundeck.

The four men climbed to the top of the roof and discovered it was not the average roof. Romans finished their roofs with stone tile for durability. If Jesus had worked with Joseph as a builder in Sephoris as is most likely, then He probably learned this advanced method of construction there (no shame in having a nice house).

The faithful friends removed the tiles,[367] broke through all that mud and brush,[368] and gave the house a new skylight. Nothing was going to stop them. Then, they let their man down... into the presence of Jesus.

Some people have let you down before. Did you let those situations bring you to Jesus? I'm sure the guy on the stretcher felt a little panic while his friends sent him through the roof. Sometimes your status quo has to be broken up for you to get to Jesus.

---

[365] See Luke 5:17.
[366] See Mark 2:3; Luke 5:18.
[367] See Luke 5:19.
[368] See Mark 2:4.

Remember, the popular notion was that sin caused a person's disease. Have you ever blown a tire and thought, "God, are you mad at me?" This quadriplegic probably lived with a constant sense of guilt that his paralysis had been caused by something he had done.

Jesus got right to the internal matter before addressing the physical issue. He told him, "Cheer up, son! Your sins are forgiven!"[369] What the paralyzed man wanted was mobility; what he needed was inner cleansing.

The real miracle came when Jesus healed the man's sin-scarred soul. Secondarily, he needed his body to be able to walk. Jesus's actions show which is more important. However, just as He forgives all our sin, so He also heals all our diseases.[370]

Yes, we look at experience and say, "But not everyone is healed." However, our definitions of life cannot flow from what we have observed or experienced. Our faith must be in the Scriptures as we come to understand the nature of the Kingdom. In His realm, there is no disease. We seek for that Heaven to manifest here on earth!

Like disease to the man's immoveable body, sin paralyzes a person spiritually. Our only hope for freedom to "move" again is for Jesus to free us from sin. This paralyzed man was not the only immobilized person in the room. The religious dudes also had a paralysis, of pride.[371]

They accused Jesus of blasphemy (making fun of God or claiming to have His power). As quickly as He had perceived faith in the disabled man's friends, the King knew the religion pros were thinking evil of Him.[372] By His spiritual perception, He

---

369 This is my paraphrase of Matthew 9:2, "Be comforted, child. Your sins have been remitted." (LITV). See also Mark 2:5 and Luke 5:20.

370 See Psalm 103:2-3.

371 See Matthew 9:3; Mark 2:6; Luke 5:21.

372 See Matthew 9:4.

could see and know their thoughts.[373] and He called out the sin that was destroying them!

He challenged them to rethink their judgmentalism: "Which is easier, to say to the paralytic, '*Your* sins are forgiven you,' or to say, 'Arise, take up your bed and walk'?"[374] Really, it is no harder to "say" either phrase.

Which one is harder work? Neither. Both are impossible. The command to be healed, however, would have a more noticeable result. Clearly, Jesus showed that more than words were at work.

How sad and amazing that they would come to be entertained by seeing His miracles but angered by the healing of the inner person. Then, He demonstrated the power within Him "that you may know"[375] His power to forgive. He would heal the man to show the critics that He had power over sin as well as disease.

He commanded the forgiven man, "Rise up and take up your cot and go to your house.[376] I wonder if Jesus told him to leave so this new believer would not get infected with the viral malice the religious people had. Immediately, the guy stood up, grabbed the mat he had been lying on, and left the scene.[377] As he went, he could not help but talk about how great God was.[378]

The big mouths shut. There was nothing left to say but "We have seen wonderful things today."[379] Now they knew.

---

373 See Mark 2:8 with Matthew 9:4 and Luke 5:22.

374 Mark 2:9, NKJV. See also Matthew 9:5; Luke 5:23.

375 Mark 2:10; Matthew 9:6; Luke 5:24, LITV.

376 Mark 2:11, LITV. See also Matthew 9:6; Luke 5:24.

377 See Mark 2:12; Matthew 9:7.

378 See Luke 5:25.

379 Luke 5:26, LITV.

While listening to critics is not always wise, we will gain something if we notice what their precise question had been. As Jews who daily affirmed their belief in only One Lord, they literally asked, "Who can forgive sins but the One God?"[380] Jesus answered, "The Son of Man."[381] His did not simply demonstrate that He too could forgive sins, but that He was the One God present in their midst, in the flesh, as a Man.

Notice what lit the wick on that intense moment: the faith of the four who carried the disabled man. As the tightly packed crowd made room for the man to make his departure, they began to give glory to God that He had given such power to humans.[382] They realized that the results were not just given to humanity but the power itself. As the disciples and multitudes follow Jesus, the insightful ones noticed this: Jesus is bringing in a new era of life for common people!

Signs and wonders illustrate things. A sign is not the building. It might tell you that you are close to the building but it is not the building.

Signs will follow those that believe.[383] If we chase after signs, we will not have the substance. Those observers said, "We've never seen anything like that!" All miracles should help us see Jesus better; any other result and they have been misunderstood.

---

[380] See Mark 2:7 and Luke 5:21.

[381] Mark 2:10, LITV.

[382] See Matthew 9:8.

[383] See Mark 16:17.

OUTCASTS INCLUDED

JESUS DID NOT JUST MINISTER to those who were pushed out of society because of their diseases. He also ministered to those who were rejects because of their social status. Everyone is at the bottom of someone's totem pole.

After another lakeside teaching session, Jesus headed back into town.[384] On His way, He passed the booth of Levi, also called Matthew.[385] The term "tax collector"[386] could refer to Levi being a man who gathered tax for Rome, a toll booth operator who charged travelers a fee, or something like a customs officer collecting duties for Herod Antipas as ships came into his tetrarchy. The latter is probably the case with Levi since he had set up shop near the lake. Peter, Andrew, James, and John would have had to pay tax to him from their fishing hauls.

Two things are certain for anyone with the "collector" label: 1) he made really good money, and 2) every Jew hated him.

---

384 See Mark 2:13.
385 See Mark 2:14; Matthew 9:9.
386 See Luke 5:27.

His fellow countrymen felt like he was a sell-out to the government. He was not a poor outcast but a rich one.

Collectors like Matt had to pay a certain amount to the government and could keep what they charged above that. We call this extortion. Perhaps you can understand His relationship to society if you have had to deal with a court case. An attorney can charge you massive fees on a case no one else will take. Many lawyers have made a bad name for their trade by charging extravagant fees and twisting the facts. Perhaps that helps you feel how the public felt about Levi.

Old Matt had to be aware of Jesus like everyone else in Capernaum was. Matthew probably had interacted with Jesus often before He came and ordered him, "Follow Me!" Like the boatmen, he dropped everything, leaving it all behind.[387]

Unlike the men who earned their living with fish, Matthew could not go back. Those fishermen could pick up their trade again someday if they chose to leave Jesus. However, no administrator would reassign a collector to his government position after he had abandoned it without good reason.

What have you dropped and left behind for Jesus? Are you willing to forsake everything and be extreme about serving Him? Or do you want a soft-and-easy, Sunday-event kind of religion?

Several years ago I built up a little business doing residential repairs and remodeling. My income averaged $40/hour and would spike to twice that on some jobs. For a 22-year-old dad, life couldn't be better. I was able to buy a piece of land and a tractor with cash. We began planning to build our family a nice home.

Then, the Lord called me to walk away from that career. He prompted my wife and I to move with our two young children sixteen hundred miles across the continent. He put a message in

---

[387] See Luke 5:28.

my mouth for His people and drew me to study the Scriptures and write.

I tried a few different things to make money in our new location. I got another business going in marketing and communications, but then one day He showed me to let that go. I walked away again.

Then after trying my hand in home remodeling again, I realized how extreme He was being. He gave me a vision of me walking behind Him, hanging onto His hand. He was walking fast and I had to hurry to keep up with Him. I saw a cliff coming up rapidly and it looked like He was about to just walk off the edge into thin air. I still held onto His hand.

Then, I looked as I followed Him off the edge and saw His feet were on a tight wire. I was committed at that point and held onto His hand for dear life. I would have lost my balance if I had not hung onto His hand.

Below, I saw several bridges under construction. Everyone was trying to cross the chasm, which symbolized life. Some were building very unsafe structures to get across. Others had rugged steel girders and diamond-tread steel surfaces. Others used wood. Some bridges were very fancy and very ornate.

I realized that everyone needs resources of some sort to make it through life. Some were getting across the journey of life with great wealth to draw on. Others were relying on the government to survive. Some were spending every hour trying to eke out enough money to bridge the gap of life. Others took out loan after loan.

Jesus, however, was not depending on any of those methods. He wanted me to walk with Him from a different starting point, a different support system, and a different destination. On the other side of the chasm, a beautiful palace of gold loomed before us.

Everyone invests themselves into this life. Their best is here and now. The tight wire Jesus walked on looked so feeble compared to everyone else's path of choice. They put all their resources into crossing the canyon. With Jesus, we invest all our resources into the destination.

I kept the vision to myself and prayed about it for understanding. I continued to obey the Lord in what He had called me to do. Then, I had a friend call me. He said at a prayer meeting some other friends asked him how I was doing. He said he hadn't heard from me since I moved away, but then he said something prophetic: "I know one thing... he's walking a thin line... but I see that he's holding onto Jesus."

I can testify that we have indeed walked a thin wire financially, yet He has faithfully and unfailingly supplied for my growing family. Recently, holding onto the hand of Jesus has led my family to sell our home and move into an RV while waiting on His next assignment. It's a long story that will be more fun to tell after the fact than while we are in it.

I can't imagine how Matt felt when he had to give his boss his resignation. I can see his family and buddies being mad at him. I remember the feeling of letting down some of the guys I had started a business with. They could go on without me, but it hurt momentum to see me abandon ship like that.

Do you feel weird about what Jesus has called you to do? Did it hurt to give up what you did? Do you think He might ask something more from you?

Matthew did not let this new turn in his life "weird out" his friends. He invited them for a feast.[388] This was an opportunity for other collectors to "come and see" Jesus.

Matt's friends came from the non-religious margins of society. Jesus shared the table with such "edgy" characters. At

---

[388] See Mark 2:15; Matthew 9:10; Luke 5:29.

that time and location, to eat at a table with someone was to make a close commitment to them. If they ever needed anything, you would be there for them. Jesus ate with sinners, committing Himself to them!

Many social outcasts began to follow Jesus. Non-religious people are more likely to be interested in the Lord Himself than the religious are. Religious people are too busy talking about what they believe rather than focusing on Jesus.

The Pharisees looked down on anyone who did not line up with their fence around the law. They had itemized extra rules to protect the written ones from Moses. Jesus invests more in reckless, don't-care-what-society-thinks people than He does the you-have-to-do-everything-my-way club.

The scribes and Pharisees saw Him eating with the "losers." They could not see Jesus, only the people they did not like. They did not complain directly to the Master, they tried to make Him look bad to His followers. They said, "Why does your teacher eat with tax collectors and sinners?"[389]

Of course, Jesus never approved of sin and spoke clearly against it. The Pharisees also had separated themselves from wickedness. But then, they used their razor-sharp moral living as an axe to chop down others. They had become so focused on their purity that they began to look down on those who did not measure up to their distinctives.

Legalists chop down others with their rules to hide their own sin. Lawless ones offer "judgment free" zones so they can hide their own sin without being judged. Both are wrong. Those who live by love overcome sin and confess when they have not.

Are you grossed out by sinful people? You have the wrong heart. You take offense at tattoos, facial piercings, or outrageous

---

389 Matthew 9:11, LITV. See also Mark 2:16; Luke 5:30.

clothing? What kind of people are you looking for, perfected ones?

The perfect are not looking for Jesus; they think they are the Messiah. You want to love the broken because they know they need a Savior. "I'm living better than this person, that addict, that sinner."

You want a measurement of whether you are more saved than someone else? The measurement of your spirituality is not in how much money you give to the local church, and you need to give. Your value is not in how much you pray, and you need to pray.

It is not going to be in how early or how often you go to church. It is not the shine of your shoes or style of your hairdo. What matters is if you get people to see Jesus. Follow Him and bring others to shore where He is.

Levi did not leave his profession just to hear stories and listen to teaching. He apprenticed to learn how to do something. We are called to Jesus to do a work for Him. Some believers do not even know what a disciple is. We have to reconnect with what the church is supposed to be.

When Jesus heard what they were saying, He made His mission clear: to recover the ones ill with sin.[390] How was a physician to do his work if he did not see the patients? Jesus must encounter the sin-diseased people or His purpose would never be fulfilled. Without saying it, Jesus just revealed Himself to them as the Great Physician—but did they see it?

He said, "Go and learn what this means: 'I desire mercy and not sacrifice.'"[391] This phrase comes from the prophet Hosea

---

[390] See Matthew 9:12; Mark 2:17; Luke 5:31.
[391] Matthew 9:13, LITV.

and reflects the true heart of the Lord.[392] God required sacrifices under the Mosaic covenant, but He also wanted the heart of humans to open up and receive others.

Often, high-sacrifice religious people run low on mercy. The Pharisees would never have eaten the food of those backsliders Jesus met with—it would be unthinkable to share food that had not been properly tithed of. Jesus's mercy looked beyond the flaws and mistakes of this crowd and showed them He loved them, not just a performance.

Jesus came to bring sinful people to turn from their old ways. The Pharisees thought they knew who those sinful people are. However, if they had been listening, Jesus just pointed out their sin of not showing mercy. Those polished pros did not think they needed His help—and that is precisely why they did not get it.

Are you the sinner or the religious pro? Do you think you have it all figured out? Or could you be guilty of their same sin?

Do you have sinner friends like Levi? Many Christians have no friends who do not know about Jesus. Religious people avoid friendships with the outcasts for fear of contamination. Yes, a weak believer can be influenced by a sinful friend. Healthy disciples of Jesus, though, make friends of sinners and help them see Jesus.

Anyone can talk about how they will do this, but true trainees of Jesus actually do it! In the next book, we will move closer to the action of being a disciple. Soon, you also will not just be chumming with religion pros but be living to call sinners to convert as Jesus did.[393]

---

[392] "For I desired mercy, and not sacrifice; and the knowledge of God more than burnt offerings." Hosea 6:6, LITV.

[393] See Matthew 9:13; Luke 5:32.

MORE THAN AN UPGRADE

JOHN THE BAPTIZER had been locked up for months at this point in the narrative. He had lived a humble life of eating wild food, wearing rough clothing, and not going to social events.[394] His followers mourned and fasted after his arrest.

Based on John's calling, all of his disciples should have become followers of Jesus. Some had, but many hadn't transferred loyalty yet. Today, amazing personalities attract their own disciples instead of leading them to Jesus. If Jesus is not the focus, the religion is defective.

The disciples of John locked step with the Pharisees on some points. They had much in common: seeking the Messiah, promoting countercultural changes, and consistency in personal discipline. One day, the two groups were not eating (fasting). This may have been the same day Jesus and His group were feasting at Matthew's house.[395]

---

[394] He was known for "neither eating or drinking" in Matthew 11:18, a reference to his avoidance of feasts and social gatherings.

[395] See Mark 2:18.

Pharisees and John's disciples came and asked why Jesus's disciples did not fast often and pray like they did.[396] They fasted on certain days of the week[397] and prayed at set times of the day. Jesus's disciples were not so pious and regimented.

Jesus challenged them, "Can the sons of the bridechamber mourn as long as the bridegroom is with them?"[398] You don't go to a wedding to mourn but rejoice (typically, anyway). Why should they have been fasting when they were in the presence of Jesus?[399] Fasting is a form of mourning; being around Jesus brought them joy.

Jesus did not condemn His followers for not fasting. He didn't force spiritual disciplines upon them. He brought them alongside Himself so they could see how a King lives. Eventually, their hearts would change so that they mourned for the same things that grieve Him. This happens within us, too.

Some versions put this phrase in the Lord's mouth as "the friends of the bridegroom."[400] Jesus calls His followers "friends." He means you. He didn't say "slaves" or "servants." He thinks of His trainees and understudies as close relationships like the traditional groomsmen in a wedding.

A groom's friends celebrate with him. Jesus's friends enjoyed their time with Him. His first disciples hung out at His house. Do you have a friendship with Jesus or a religious discipline?

The Pharisees and disciples of John came to Him on a religious level. For most "Christians," Jesus is a creed, a doctrinal battle, or a badge they wear. The Pharisees didn't value personal

---

[396] See Matthew 9:14; Luke 5:33.
[397] See Luke 18:12.
[398] Matthew 9:15, LITV.
[399] See Matthew 9:15; Mark 2:19; Luke 5:34.
[400] Matthew 9:15, NKJV.

closeness with the Lord as a factor in the faith. They focused their devotion on looking for the right things to do and to find more ways of doing them righter. They were not the Groom's friends. The "sinners" were.

Is Jesus in your friendship list? I know He's already in your spiritual sector of life. He's probably on your schedule (church services, prayer times, and so on). But is He top of your friends list?

I'm not asking if you talk to Him. The question is what do you talk to Him about? Are your conversations with Him theological or problem-focused? Like with the woman at the well, He wants into our personal lives, close enough to heal our hurts.

The disciples of John continue to remind me how quickly one can go from being an energetic follower to being a religious traditionalist. They thought Jesus should make the disciples give up eating on certain days of the week.[401] That's how religion works. It makes you do stuff to fit in, measure up, or somehow prove yourself.

Jesus would not force His disciples to go without eating. John's disciples had only been around for a year or so and already they were legalistic and judgmental like the doomed Pharisees. You might have a programmed religion, too. If you lose sight of Jesus, you slip into a rut about what you do rather than Who you know.

"Don't worry," Jesus was saying. His disciples would fast when He was ripped away from them.[402] Someone who follows Jesus will fast and pray. In the next book, we will see how they learn this and it is far different from the regimented, you-have-to-do-this religious exercises and "spiritual disciplines" some like to force on others.

---

[401] See Luke 5:34.
[402] See Mark 2:20; Matthew 9:15; Luke 5:35.

Imagine being at a wedding and someone kidnapped the groom. That would kill the party and everyone would be in a state of shock. The bride would grieve. That's the state of the church today. Instead of fasting as a ritual for self-justification, both Jesus's first disciples and we mourn that we cannot see Jesus in the flesh. We cannot wait until He shows up.

This conversation about personal spiritual disciplines prompts Jesus to explain why we need a factory reset, not just an upgrade. Well, they didn't have phones then, so He couldn't use that analogy. Instead, He used one His audience would have understood much better.

He said, "And no one sews a patch of unmilled cloth on an old garment, else it takes away its fullness, the new from the old, and a worse tear occurs."[403] What does He imply? Start over with a whole piece of cloth rather than just scab your life together.

As a boy, my mom patched holes in the knees of my pants. The patch was always darker than my faded jeans. Somehow I wore out the upper half of the pant leg, not just the knee. Thus, the cloth above the patch would tear soon. At times, we added another patch on top of a patch, but the old, thin cloth would rip above the patch again.

Jesus used that idea of a knee patch, or something like it, to illustrate the difference between what He was doing and what the religion pros were doing. Syncretism is the attempt to merge multiple ideologies together. Jesus was not attempting to meld their program with His Kingdom. John's disciples and the Pharisees were trying to get Jesus's peeps to blend with their ways.

Modern Christianity has many patches with different patterns of thinking all loosely sewn together with a thin thread. I have worked with inmates who had developed a bapti-catho-

---

403 Mark 2:21, LITV. See also Matthew 9:16; Luke 5:36.

mormo-jehova-musli-costal religion. They believed a little bit of everything they heard from all the volunteers who came through.

Some of the popular Christian speakers and authors today blend satanic self-glorifying talk with Bible verses. Churches should not be spouting humanism, eastern religion, or pop psychology. The whole garment gets ripped up. You cannot patch Jesus into what you are already doing. We must let Him reset everything we know and value.

Jesus used another illustration to make this gigantic point about making disciples and the work of His Kingdom: "And no one puts new wine into old skins; otherwise, the new wine will burst the skins, and it will be poured out, and the skins will perish. But new wine is to be put into new skins, and both are preserved together."[404]

When fermenting wine, one did not use an old skin. In that time, the skin from the whole body of a goat became a wine flask. They would sew the openings shut and cork one leg to use as a pour spout. A fresh goat hide would flex and stretch with the pressure caused by fermentation. An already-stretched-out leather bottle would burst if new wine fermented in it.

Religious methods, structures, and traditions do not make a usable container for the work of Jesus. His Kingdom is the structure, not the synagogue or the Pharisee traditions.

If you try to pour the power of the Spirit and the life of Christ into programmed religion, both will be lost. Many today can be filled with the Spirit and shortly afterward their whole world falls apart. The institution, tradition, old life could not hold the new thing God was doing.

It is hard for people who are used to a tradition to change. Literally translated, the drinkers of old wine think "the old is

----

[404] Luke 5:37-38, LITV. See also Matthew 9:17; Mark 2:22.

good."[405] They have no thirst for something new because their old ways fit them well.

So many Christians "got saved" so they could be evacuated by Jesus someday (go to heaven), but they don't care to know Him now. They are comfortable in their traditions. They have not changed at the core of their desires, motivations, and objectives in life.

What fills you? Jesus did not come to tank us up with pride or deluge us with more denominations. He does not wish to pour His Spirit into those with practiced behaviors. We don't bring Jesus our old hide to be patched up with a few better behaviors. We give Him our impulses and agendas.

John prepped his disciples to see Jesus, but their old religious ideas blinded them from trying the new wine. No wonder Jesus invested in outcasts. Only a few religious people desired the Kingdom and surrendered to His whole new world.

The disciples hadn't yet experienced whole-cloth conversion. They were not new wineskins yet. Once that happened, they would begin to fast, pray, and give. Personal disciplines are not personal if we only do them because someone made us do it.

At one point, I thought it was my job as a dad to tell our children they needed to fast. I remember being so hungry for the things of God at age thirteen that I begged my parents to let me fast. They were worried about my health and feared that going without eating might stunt growth during those developmental years so they would only let me fast one day at a time. I think I was fifteen before they finally let me fast for three days.

So, I thought it was important for my children's spiritual development to fast. I did not force it on the young ones and I didn't really force it on the older ones. I did talk about it in such a

---

405 See Luke 5:39.

way as to make them feel their faith was defective if they didn't fast. So, they were manipulated into fasting because of my convictions, not their own.

My wife talked with me about this, pointing out that if our teenagers were skipping meals just for me, then they were not doing it for the Lord. I was treating these young disciples the way John's disciples treated Jesus's newbies. I couldn't see it. I thought she was wrong—they needed to fast at young ages like I had wanted to.

Then I had a dream. I hate it when Jesus and my wife team up on me. In my dream I was on something like a high school running track. My family was near me, too. I took off running but they were kind of playing around, not competing. I ran circles around them and refused to stop because I knew there was a big prize if I did. Then I realized, they did not know what the prize was.

I woke up. I immediately knew what it meant. They wouldn't fast like I do until they understood what was to be gained by fasting. I dropped the pressure for them to have a weekly planned famine. I wanted them to do it for Jesus, not me.

Instead of focusing on such requirements, we focused more on seeing Jesus correctly and understanding His Kingdom. With time, I noticed that the Lord would call them to fast at times when others were eating. They might not do it the way I do or when I do, but they are learning the value of the reward. That internal motivation will take a person much farther than any guilt induced disciplines ever could.

In the next book, we will see how Jesus teaches about these things. His words have set me back on the right track. I'll see you there soon.

It is so important we learn the genuine and not the counterfeit. If we are going to be true disciples, we have to have the whole Jesus and not just some parts we like. We have to become new creatures in Him.

What are some "old skins" you may have been thinking you could pour Jesus into? What would your heart look like if you started over from scratch? As you see Jesus better and better, be prepared for a total makeover of your life. When the Lord pours the new wine (the Spirit) into new you (your converted heart), both will last.

There is a lot we are learning from Jesus and it has only begun: new thinking, new faith, new birth, and a new source of life. As we continue following Jesus in the Gospels, we will see Him establish the code for how a transformed person thinks and lives. Are you ready for a solid, unshakeable life?

Meet me in the next book called *Live Above* as Jesus teaches us to overcome rejection, live the way the King does, and pray in a way that changes the world.

APPENDIX

"Alcohol in the Bible"

WAS JESUS ENDORSING or supplying drunkness? No. Here's why.

The distilled liquors we think of today and the fermented wine they used then stand two millennia apart. Jesus did not bring His crew to "come and see" a drinking party. The wine they served would have been like punch at a wedding today. This is not to say it had zero alcohol content, but that it was much less than a wine would have today and I can explain why.

Jews fermented grape juice to preserve it and use throughout the year. They did not have frozen concentrates like we use today but used this thick, fermented concentrate. One did not just open a flask and drink it.

When ready to use, they diluted with a ratio of 4 parts water to 1 part fermented pulp. Today, frozen grape juice concentrates are mixed at a ration of 3:1. Romans were known to dilute their wine as much as 9:1. Diluted wine like this would have only a minimal amount of alcohol, such as one might find in kombucha today.

Drinking fluids with such active agents in them helped offset any impurities or bacteria present in the water they drank, since much of it could be ground-sourced.[406] Some Jews went so far as to evaporate alcohol from their wine by heating it before diluting it and serving it. Very possibly, this event contained no alcohol.

The guests at the event and the first readers of this story would not assume this was an event where people were getting drunk. This was a very devout family. In a minute we will see that they were devoted to pure lives and doing everything they knew to live holy lives. Such a family would have been ashamed for anyone to think they would be drinking like the heathens.[407]

Now that I have relieved my concern that someone might use this episode to justify an addiction, remember the point was for the reader to see what worried Mary. First-century weddings were much more than just cake, punch, and dinner mints. And they took longer than an afternoon. The lack of wedding beverage would cripple the event.

---

[406] This makes sense when we read Paul's instructions to Timothy to not just drink water but also use a "little wine" for the sake of his stomach, in I Timothy 5:23.

[407] Devout people took the words of Proverbs 20:1 and 23:20-21, 29-35 literally. It should be unthinkable to followers of Jesus to be given to alcohol as well. See Romans 13:13; I Corinthians 5:11; 6:10; Ephesians 5:18; I Peter 4:3-4. Of course, there is the statement in John 2:10 of "when they have drunk freely" (LITV) which could be translated as "when the guests are drunk" (NET Bible). However, even if the latter is the proper understanding of this statement, it was a generalized idea and did not pertain specifically to this feast.

BIBLIOGRAPHY

Beasley-Murray, George R. *John*. 2nd ed. Word Biblical Comentary 36. Nashville: Nelson, 1999.

Bock, Darrell. *Luke*. Vol 1. Baker Exegetical Commentary on the New Testament. Grand Rapids, MI: Baker Academic, 1994.

_____. *Luke*. NIV Application Commentary. Grand Rapids, MI: Zondervan, 1996.

Briscoe, Stuart. *Flowing Streams*. Grand Rapids, MI: Zondervan, 2008.

Burge, Gary M. *John*. NIV Application Commentary. Grand Rapids, MI: Zondervan, 2000.

Hull, Bill. *Jesus Christ Disciple Maker*. Grand Rapids, MI: Revell, 1984.

France, R. T. *Matthew: An Introduction and Commentary*. Vol. I. Leon Morris, Ed. Downers Grove, IL: Intervarsity, 1985.

_____. *The Gospel of Matthew*. New International Commentary on the New Testament. Grand Rapids, MI: Eerdmans, 2007.

Keener, Craig. *The Gospel of John*. Vol. I. Peabody, MA: Hendrickson, 2003.

_____. *The Gospel of Matthew: A Social-Rhetorical Commentary*. Grand Rapids, MI: Eerdmans, 2009.

Kruse, Colin. *John: An Introduction and Commentary*. Downers Grove, IL: InterVarsity, 2003.

Moffic, Evan. *What Every Christian Needs to Know about the Jewishness of Jesus*. Nashville: Abingdon, 2015.

Morris, Leon. *Luke: An Introduction and Commentary*. Tyndale New Testament Commentaries. Vol. 3. Downers Grove, IL: 1988.

Wilkins, Michael J. *Matthew*. NIV Application Commentary. Grand Rapids, MI: Zondervan, 2004.

ABOUT THE AUTHOR

DANIEL J. KOREN has written for a variety of magazines, teaching curriculums, and other resources that help people expand their biblical understanding and personal growth. With over one million words in print, Daniel's goal is to give away one million ebooks.

Currently, he has focused his time and efforts on getting people to see the Kingdom of God. This includes books, study guides, and teaching tools covering every verse of the New Testament. In his free time, Daniel enjoys reading (and smelling) thick reference books, working with his children and wife Leanne, and building relationships with those who want Jesus first in everything.

The Journey has Begun

WE HAVE BEGUN THE ADVENTURE! Are you committed to the Kingdom life? The next book *Live Above* dives into how Jesus handled troublemakers and how He trained His disciples to live differently (than the established religions were doing).

In the next volume, learn from Jesus:

- how to deal with rejection,
- how Kingdom citizens interact with each other,
- how to establish the Kingdom on earth,
- to avoid the gears of the religious machine, and
- how to pray in a way that changes the world.

See you in book three of the Jesus in 20/20 series!

www.ingramcontent.com/pod-product-compliance
Lightning Source LLC
Chambersburg PA
CBHW031251090426
42742CB00007B/405

* 9 7 8 0 9 7 9 5 2 9 1 7 7 *